TAKE CONTROL OF DYSLEXIA AND OTHER READING DIFFICULTIES

The Ultimate Guide for Kids

Jennifer Engel Fisher
& Janet Price

PRUFROCK PRESS INC.
WACO, TEXAS

TAKE CONTROL OF DYSLEXIA AND OTHER READING DIFFICULTIE

Library of Congress Cataloging-in-Publication Data

Fisher, Jennifer Engel, 1970-
Take control of dyslexia and other reading difficulties : the ultimate guide for kids / by Jennifer Engel Fisher and Janet Price.
    p. cm.
    Includes bibliographical references.
    ISBN 978-1-59363-748-4 (pbk.)
    1. Dyslexia--Juvenile literature. 2. Reading disability--Juvenile literature. 3. Reading--Remedial teaching--Juvenile literature. I. Price, Janet, 1964- II. Title.
    LB1050.5.F547 2012
    371.91'44--dc23

                        2011040940

Edited by Lacy Compton
Cover and layout design by Raquel Trevino

ISBN-13: 978-1-59363-748-4

Printed in the United States of America.

At the time of this book's publication, all facts and figures cited are the most current available. All telephone numbers, addresses, and website URLs are accurate and active. All publications, organizations, websites, and other resources exist as described in the book, and all have been verified. The author and Prufrock Press Inc. make no warranty or guarantee concerning the information and materials given out by organizations or content found at websites, and we are not responsible for any changes that occur after this book's publication. If you find an error, please contact Prufrock Press Inc.

Prufrock Press Inc.
P.O. Box 8813
Waco, TX 76714-8813
Phone: (800) 998-2208
Fax: (800) 240-0333
http://www.prufrock.com

DEDICATION

I dedicate this book to my in-laws, Barbara and Larry Fisher, who have always treated me like their daughter. And, to my sons, Brett and Ethan, who make me smile every day.
— Jennifer

I dedicate this book to Nancy and Marty Price, my mother-in-law and father-in-law, whom I've known now half my life. Thank you for being a constant source of strength, reason, and support.
— Janet

CONTENTS

ACKNOWLEDGEMENTS

There are many people we wish to thank who have been so helpful and supportive throughout this process.

First and foremost, we'd like to thank our editor, Lacy Compton, who is an author's dream to work with. As always, we are thankful for the professional mentorship and personal friendship of Rich Weinfeld, Director of Weinfeld Education Group, as well as the entire staff of WEG. We are grateful to be working in a field where we can all make a difference in the lives of families and kids with special needs.

Thank you to several private schools in the Washington, D.C., metropolitan area for allowing us to survey their students about reading difficulties. We wish to thank the Chelsea School in Silver Spring, MD, Debbie Lourie in particular. We also wish to thank the Siena School in Silver Spring, MD, and especially Bekah Atkinson and Clay

Kaufman. Thank you to all of the kids and teens who partici- pated in our online survey and who allowed us to interview them. We couldn't have done it without you! A special shout- out goes to a sixth grader from Maryland who supplied us with great information for our chapter on writing.

A special thank you to Dr. Linda Spencer for her feed- back on an early chapter in this book and for her continued support of our work, and to Dr. Joyce Cooper-Kahn and Dr. Laurie Dietzel for their expertise on executive functioning. We are very grateful.

Thank you as well to Joan Green, for her input on our technology chapter. We appreciate Joan's important contri- bution to understanding the field of assistive technology.

Thank you to Devon Kesterman, photographer extraor- dinaire, for making us look good.

We also wish to thank the important contributors to the field of dyslexia and reading research who came before us, as well as to acknowledge the seminal work of Sally Shaywitz, M.D.

Finally, no acknowledgement section would be com- plete without grateful thanks for the love and support of our husbands and children: Noel, Ethan, and Brett Fisher and Richard, Benjamin, and Lauren Price.

INTRODUCTION
Why Should I Read This Book, Anyway?

There are lots of books out there about dyslexia and other reading difficulties. There are books that explain reading difficulties to your parents, and books to help your teachers understand ways to help you. There are reading workbooks with activities to do. This book is different from all of those. This book is written just for you.

You hate to read, because it's hard. You probably didn't even pick out this book yourself, did you? Maybe a parent or a teacher gave it to you. Maybe you're listening to it on a CD or through a text-to-speech program. That's okay. By the time you finish this book, whether you are reading it or someone is reading it to you, you will have something you didn't have before. You will have a better understanding of how you learn, and you will have a plan of attack to take control of your reading difficulties.

Right now, the only thing you may know about reading is that you're not good at it, you don't like it, and everyone else seems to think it's easy. That may make you feel frustrated, angry, or discouraged. So it might surprise you to learn that "reading is not a natural or instinctive process" (Shaywitz, 2003, p 9). Nobody is born automatically being able to read; everyone needs to be taught. Why, then, is it easy for lots of kids and not so easy for you? Part of the problem is that everyone starts out being taught to read in the same way, but for some people, this doesn't match the way their brains learn. In fact, dyslexia affects as many as one out of five children. That means there are about 10 million American kids who have trouble learning to read (Shaywitz, 2003). You are not alone!

> **Nobody is born automatically being able to read. Everyone has to *learn* how to read.**

To prove it, this book also includes helpful comments from kids and teens all over the country who have dyslexia or other reading difficulties. Their names have been changed to protect their privacy, but their stories and observations will probably seem very familiar to you.

As you make your way through this book, you will also learn about strategies. A strategy is like a plan of attack. It can take many forms, from simple tips and tricks, to cutting-edge assistive technology. The more you learn about how your brain learns, the more strategies you can identify that will help you.

This book begins by explaining what it really means to read. Did you know that there are five elements to reading? Not only that, but there are also four different methods of learning. You're going to find out all about those and more!

➤ In Chapter 1, you will learn that reading isn't so simple after all, but it's also nothing to be afraid of.

➤ Chapter 2 will teach you about dyslexia and other reading difficulties. What are the learning differences that are getting in your way? How can understanding these differences help you?

➤ Chapter 3 will teach you about self-advocacy. What does it mean to "take control"? How do other kids feel about asking for help, and what works for them?

➤ Chapter 4 will describe the different ways people learn, and introduce you to "metacognition," or learning about learning.

➤ Chapter 5 offers reading strategies that can help you.

➤ Chapter 6 will discuss the exciting options available through assistive technology.

➤ Chapter 7 will talk about the connection between reading and writing.

➤ Chapter 8 will summarize the strategies you learned about in the previous chapters and include questions to help you remember them.

Reading is an important skill that touches on nearly every aspect of life. Dyslexia and other reading difficulties may seem overwhelming. Hopefully this book will help you to understand why you learn the way you do, and what strategies you can use to take control of your reading difficulties.

CHAPTER 1

WHAT DOES IT MEAN TO READ?

You can ask a million different people what it means to read and get a million different answers. Here are some responses from middle and high school students when asked what it means to read:

Sam, age 14: "I think it means you see the words and comprehend them and think about them through thought, memory, knowledge, and understanding."
Hannah, age 12: "To learn what you need."
Michelle, age 16: "To be able to look at anything with words on it and be able to pronounce the words that are present."

As you can see, the three students above all have different definitions of what it means to read. In this chapter you will learn the actual definition of reading and learn about the purposes of reading. Even though it can be difficult, we really do need to learn how to read.

"I am never going to learn how to read," Rebecca said after coming off the bus. *"Aisha can read everything and the teacher always calls on her. It's not fair. What's wrong with me?"* Rebecca has every right to feel this way. Reading can be harder for some people than others. Just like with music, sports, or art, some kids pick things up faster than others. There are many steps to reading that can be confusing, from identifying the letters of the alphabet to matching that letter to a sound. Some letters look alike, such as "m" and "n" or "I" and "l," which makes it even harder to figure out. Once you know your letters and sounds, you then have to work on putting the sounds together, then words, then sentences, and then

What does it mean to read?

"I think it means you see the words and comprehend them and think about them through thought, memory, knowledge, and understanding."—Sam, age 14

you have to understand what you are reading. It's amazing how many skills are needed in order to read.

WHY DO WE READ?

There are three main purposes for reading. We read for information, we read for enjoyment, and we read to complete a task. So why do we do it? We read in order to survive. We read to help ourselves and others. We read to learn. We read for knowledge, and we read for our jobs and school.

> **Why do we read?**
> ➤ **for information**
> ➤ **for enjoyment**
> ➤ **to complete a task**

WE READ FROM THE BRAIN

Before we get deep into the parts of reading, let's find out how the brain reads. Reading relies on the part of the brain that processes receptive language. Receptive language is just a fancy way of saying that you understand what is being said to you. For typical readers, the brain "reads" when we are able to use the parts of the brain that process the visual features of numbers and letters (like lines and shapes), then connect them to form words and then meaning.

THE ELEMENTS OF READING

In 2000, the National Reading Panel (NRP) of the National Institute of Child Health and Human Development (NICHD) issued a report that identified five areas that were critical for effective reading instruction. It may seem to you like reading is just one task, but the truth is there are five essential elements of reading:

1. phonemic awareness;
2. phonics;
3. reading fluency, including oral reading skills;
4. vocabulary; and
5. reading comprehension.

Did you know that there are five essential elements of reading?

Phonemic awareness is the first stage and the most important piece of reading and spelling (Shaywitz, 2003). Phonemic awareness is your ability to hear, identify, and put together phonemes, which are the smallest units of sound. For example, when you hear the word "cat," if you have phonemic awareness, you are able to identify the three sounds of the word: /k/, /a/, and /t/. Decoding is another word you will hear in connection with phonemic awareness, and probably one you'll hear your teacher use a lot, too. Decoding is the process of breaking words apart into their individual sounds, and encoding is putting the sounds back together to form words. One test for phonemic awareness is to give the student three sounds and then blend them together to form a word. That is an example of encoding.

Phonics is the system of teaching the relationships between letters and sounds in language. When you realize that the letter T produces the sound /t/ as in tap, that is phonics. Only about 80% of our language follows phonetic rules, which means 20% of the time, a word will be an exception to the rule. That can make it even more challenging for those with reading difficulties to learn how to read and then apply those rules when writing.

Reading fluency is the third element of reading. It is the ability to read phrases and sentences smoothly and with a reasonable speed, and, at the same time, understand what it is that you are reading. Those with dyslexia commonly have weaknesses in reading fluency. Putting together words into meaningful phrases is difficult. Decoding errors may also slow down reading fluency. If you are spending too much time sounding out the words, you may lose the meaning of the text, causing problems with reading comprehension.

The fourth element of reading is vocabulary. Vocabulary refers to the words we must know in order to communicate effectively. It applies to speaking, listening, reading, and writing. Vocabulary often predicts how good a person's reading comprehension will be, which makes sense if you think about it. After all, if you don't know the meaning of a word, how can you understand what you are reading? Remember this the next time your teacher assigns lists of vocabulary words for homework!

Reading comprehension is the fifth element of reading. It refers to the ability to understand what you are reading. Reading comprehension pulls together all of the other four elements of reading, because in order to understand what you are reading, you need to have phonemic awareness, phonics skills, fluency, and vocabulary. There are two types of reading comprehension, literal and inferential. Literal comprehension is the factual information that is right there in the text. You can think of literal comprehension as the wh- questions of who, what, where, and when. The other wh- question, why, is an inferential question. Inferential comprehension is sometimes called "reading between the lines." It requires the reader to draw conclusions and rely on personal experiences and relate them to the text. A student who has a difficult time understanding cause and effect, forming conclusions, and seeing things from a character's point of view will have difficulty with inferential comprehension. Finally, a question beginning with the word "How" can be either literal or inferential.

WHAT ARE PURPOSES AND GENRES?

Purposes and genres are two more terms that you will hear in connection with reading. Purposes are *why* we read, and genres are *what* we read. We read for a variety of purposes:

➤ for information such as in nonfiction books and dictionaries,

➤ to perform a task such as in recipes and how-to manuals, and

➤ for literary experience such as in the books you read for fun or because you're interested in the topic.

Every person gravitates toward a certain genre or kind of text. From poetry to nonfiction, people have different preferences. It should not come as a surprise that a student who has difficulty with inferential comprehension may be more likely to enjoy nonfiction texts, where most of the information is literal. Biographies are an example of a nonfiction text. Just because some genres may be easier, don't rule the other ones out. You can use strategies such as books on tape to help you understand other text. Two teens told us some of their purposes for reading:

Sarah, age 13: "Sometimes it (reading) is fun if I like the book and if I can see the words that I am reading."

Michael, age 16: "I personally am your average lazy teen, so obviously I much rather prefer video games and other unhealthy things that are killing neurons, but I do turn to reading as a last resort usually. For example, every night, if I can't fall asleep, I read a very boring book to make me sleepy."

Why do you read?

"Sometimes it (reading) is fun if I like the book and if I can see the words that I am reading."—Sarah, age 13

HOW WORDS ARE PUT TOGETHER SO WE CAN PULL THEM APART

Approximately 84% of the English language follows phonics rules, which makes decoding the other 16% impossible (Seipel, 2010). Research shows that phonics is the most effective method of teaching reading. There are 44 phonemes that make up the English language. Those phonemes fall into the six types of syllables we have that help us to decode, or pull apart, unknown words. The six types of syllables are:

1. *Closed Syllable*: When a vowel is "closed in" with a consonant to its right, making the vowel sound short. Examples include "cat," "up," and "last."

2. *Open Syllable*: When a vowel is to the right of a consonant, the vowel sounds long. This syllable type is typically found at the end of a word. Examples include "go" and "me."

3. *Vowel-Consonant-e Syllable*: Otherwise known as the magic-e rule, it is when the vowel *e* follows a closed syllable, making the vowel before the consonant sound long. Examples include "cake," "side," and "hope."

4. *Vowel Team Syllable*: When there are two vowels next to each other that make a new single sound. Examples include "moat," "beat," and "paint."

5. *Consonant-le Syllable*: When a consonant such as *b* is followed by *le*. Examples include "candle," "able," and "edible."

6. *R-Controlled Syllable*: When a vowel is followed by the letter *r*. The *r* "controls" the vowel and changes the way it is pronounced. Examples include "tar," "her," and "blur."

Learning the six types of syllables is a key element of reading. The next step is to figure out how to recognize the syllable type and determine if there are more than one type of syllable type in a multisyllabic word. A syllable is defined as a word or part of a word that has a vowel you can hear. In the following chapters, you will learn how to identify the type of syllable as well as how to divide words into syllables.

BLENDS, DIGRAPHS, AND DIPHTHONGS, HUH?

You have probably heard your teacher talk about blends, digraphs, and diphthongs. What funny words! In order to understand the process of reading, you need to understand what they are.

A blend is when two or more consonants are next to each other so that you hear both of their sounds when read. For example, *bl*, *gr*, *fl*, and *str* are common blends. Consonant digraphs are when two or more consonants next to each other form a new sound. For example, *th*, *sh*, *ch*, and *tch* are consonant digraphs. Vowel digraphs are when two vowels are next to each other and you only hear the sound of the first letter. We like to remember this rule as "two vowels go walking, the first one does the talking." For example, this shows up when *ai* makes the long /a/ sound as in the word "main" and when *oa* makes the long /o/ sound in the word "coat." Diphthongs are when two vowels next to each other form one new sound. For example, *ea*, *ie*, and *ou* are diphthongs.

PREFIXES, SUFFIXES, AND ROOTS, OH MY!

Many words are made up of a root, or base word, and a prefix. A prefix is a syllable that comes before a root word and has meaning. Suffixes are syllables with meanings that come at the end of the word. Learning common prefixes, roots, and suffixes makes decoding much easier. Common prefixes include *un-*, *pre-*, and *re-*. Common suffixes include *-ing*, *-er*, and *-ed*.

WHAT'S IN A BOOK?

Just like there is more to reading than decoding each word, there is also more to a book than just the words printed on the page. Besides the words, a book is also made up of text features. Authors use text features to organize and highlight information and to help the reader understand important concepts. Text features also include the way in which information is laid out or presented to the reader. For example, you may notice that this book is printed in a font that is larger than most books, with more white space between the lines. This is to help make it easier to track the words when you are reading.

Other text features that you will find in this book are:

➤ *Table of Contents*: A table of contents lists the chapters and pages in the book so that you can preview what you will learn and locate information easily.

➤ *Chapter Titles*: Some books only give numbers to chapters. Others, like this one, also have titles so that you have an idea what a chapter will be about before you even read it.

➤ *Headings in Bold Print*: These subheadings divide the information into different topics that relate to the main idea of the chapter.

➤ *Words in Bold Print or Italics*: When a word is highlighted in bold or italic printing, this is a signal to you that it is important.

➤ *Reference Sources in Parentheses*: When information in a nonfiction book like this one is quoted from another source, you will see that source in parentheses in the text. The reference may include the author, title, page number, and publication date of the book where the information was found or may list the website or article if the information was retrieved online or from a magazine or newspaper. You can use this information to research more about the topic.

➤ *References and Resources Sections*: More complete information about sources is also contained in the references and resources sections at the end of the book.

➤ *Definition Boxes*: Boxed information on the sides of the book is a way to highlight important ideas or information so that the reader is sure to notice.

➤ *Charts, Graphs, and Illustrations*: Until now, you may have considered the illustrations in a book to be the fun part, but believe it or not, they also have the purpose of explaining things. In nonfiction books, charts and graphs help teach you information by presenting it in a different format. In fiction books, illustrations help to show you what's going on in the story and can even provide you with clues to figure out words you have trouble reading.

➤ *Review Questions*: The last chapter of this book consists of questions to help you remember and review what you have learned.

➤ *Bulleted Lists*: When you see a list just like this one, you know that you are about to learn a group of facts related to the main idea—in this case, the main idea of the list is "What is a text feature?"

There are even more text features than the ones listed above, but this list is a good start to get you thinking about how a book gives you information in ways other than just with its words.

Picture This:
What Does It Mean to Read?

Essential Element of Reading	Definition
phonemic awareness	your ability to hear, identify, and put together phonemes, which are the smallest units of sound
phonics	the system of teaching the relationships between letters and sounds in language
reading fluency	the ability to read phrases and sentences smoothly and with a reasonable speed, and, at the same time, understand what it is that you are reading
vocabulary	the words you must know in order to communicate effectively
reading comprehension	the ability to understand what you are reading

Purposes = why we read
Genres = what we read

The purposes of reading are:
- ➤ for information such as in nonfiction books and dictionaries,
- ➤ to perform a task such as in recipes and how-to manuals, and
- ➤ for literary experience such as in the books you read for fun or because you're interested in the topic.

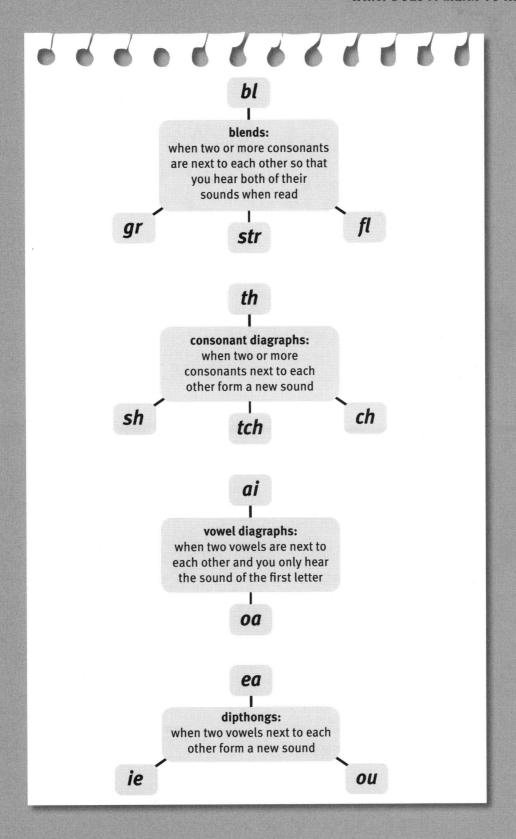

bl

blends:
when two or more consonants
are next to each other so that
you hear both of their
sounds when read

gr   **str**   **fl**

th

consonant diagraphs:
when two or more
consonants next to each
other form a new sound

sh   **tch**   **ch**

ai

vowel diagraphs:
when two vowels are next to
each other and you only hear
the sound of the first letter

oa

ea

dipthongs:
when two vowels next to each
other form a new sound

ie   **ou**

CHAPTER 2

WHAT IS A READING DISABILITY?

n the last chapter, you learned how many different steps there are in the process of reading. A reading disability is when something gets in the way of one or more of those steps, preventing you from learning to read the way most people do. This doesn't mean that you can't learn to read. It just means that you need to be taught in a way that matches up with how you learn.

WHAT IS DYSLEXIA?

You may have heard of a learning disability called dyslexia. When most people hear this word, they think of reversing letters or numbers or of letters or words floating around on the page. That's not entirely true. Dyslexia is a language-based learning disability that includes many aspects of reading.

The definition of dyslexia has changed over time, along with our understanding of it. In Greek, the prefix "dys" means defective, and "lexia" means the use of words. So if you look at the literal meaning of dyslexia, or the translation from its Greek roots, you can think of having dyslexia as having a problem with the use of words. Dyslexia is not new. One description of dyslexia that dates back to the 1800s is "word blindness." More recently, dyslexia has been described as a "word-level reading disability" (Fletcher, Lyon, Fuchs, & Barnes, 2007, p. 85). In 2002, the International Dyslexia Association Board of Directors agreed on a definition of dyslexia. The definition is a little complicated, but we will break it down piece by piece so that

dyslexia: a language-based learning disability that includes many aspects of reading

you can understand exactly what it means. The whole thing reads,

> Dyslexia is a specific learning disorder that is neurological in origin and is characterized by difficulties with accurate or fluent word recognition, and by poor spelling and decoding abilities. These difficulties typically result from a deficit in the phonological component of language that is often unexpected in relation to other cognitive abilities and the provision of effective classroom instruction. Secondary consequences may include problems in reading comprehension and reduced reading experience that can impede growth of vocabulary and background knowledge. (International Dyslexia Association, 2002, para. 1)

That is a lot of information to understand, so let's break it down:

➤ "A specific learning disorder that is neurological in origin" means having to do with the way your brain works.

➤ "Characterized by difficulties with accurate or fluent word recognition, and by poor spelling and decoding abilities" means the parts of the reading process, covered in the last chapter, where you have problems.

➤ "These difficulties typically result from a deficit in the phonological component of language" means that the trouble you have with reading is because you are having problems understanding how the sounds of language relate to what is written on the page.

➤ "That is often unexpected in relation to other cognitive abilities and the provision of effective classroom instruction" means that the difficulty experienced with reading is not something anyone would have expected, because you are otherwise smart and capable.

➤ "Secondary consequences may include problems in reading comprehension and reduced reading experience that can impede growth of vocabulary and background knowledge" means that because you are having difficulty decoding words, it can have a rippling effect and cause other reading-related problems. For example, because you have difficulty reading, you may read less, which means you are not exposed to as much vocabulary and information as your classmates.

Whatever name you give to them, the reading difficulties that you experience do not mean that you are lazy or stupid. Remember, part of the definition of dyslexia says that your reading difficulties are unexpected because you are smart and capable in other areas. Most people with dyslexia and other reading disabilities are born with them, so you shouldn't feel like you're not trying hard enough or that this is somehow your fault. Hopefully it will be a relief for you to find out that you are just as smart as anyone else, and you are probably working harder than most of your friends when it comes to reading, even if you aren't yet experiencing success.

> Remember, most people with dyslexia and other reading disabilities are born with them. You shouldn't feel like you don't try hard enough or that it is somehow your fault.

WHAT ELSE MAKES READING DIFFICULT?

The three categories of reading disabilities are reading decoding, reading fluency, and reading comprehension. These are the three important areas that people with dyslexia or other reading disabilities might have trouble with. Let's consider them one by one.

You learned about decoding in the last chapter, also called phonological awareness, or understanding what groups of letters make which sounds. How do sounds relate to a written word? When you hear someone say a word you know, for example, "book," you will get an image of that word in your mind and understand right away what it is. By the time most kids get to kindergarten, they are able to do something else with the word. They can hear the individual consonant and vowel sounds, especially the ones at the beginning and end of the word. When they learn to read a word off the page, they recognize that the letters of the written word stand for the sounds that they hear when someone speaks the word out loud. Not every child is able to hear all of the sounds in the words, though, even if they are able to get that mental image when the word is spoken. Students who are unable to distinguish the consonants and vowels as the word is spoken are very likely to have difficulty learning to read the words when they see them printed on the page. The flip side of decoding is called encoding. Just like you might have trouble decoding, or pulling a word apart, you can also have trouble encoding, or putting the word together to spell it correctly. So in addition to reading, spelling is also affected when you have difficulties with word recognition and phonological awareness, or associating sounds with letters.

Reading fluency means to read accurately, at an appropriate rate, and with appropriate tone of voice (inflection). Having dyslexia or word recognition difficulties can slow down

phonological awareness: understanding what groups of letters make which sounds

encoding: putting a word together to spell it correctly

reading, because you are not automatically and quickly recognizing words on the page. You need to stop and decode, or figure out, the words. Sometimes, a person can have difficulty with reading fluency even if he doesn't have trouble decoding. This can happen to kids who have attention problems like ADHD. It can also happen to kids with autism spectrum disorders, such as Asperger's syndrome, who may have difficulty using or understanding the proper tone of voice or inflection to indicate meaning.

Reading comprehension means understanding what you have just read. As you learned in the last chapter, there is actually more to understanding than just knowing the meaning of each word, although that is certainly a part of it. You need to know how the words are put together to form meaning. Reading comprehension also includes understanding the genre, or type of text, you are reading, and the purpose, which was reviewed in the last chapter. Are you reading for information, reading to perform a task, or reading for literary experience (fun)? Is what you are reading fiction or nonfiction? Or is it a poem? Reading comprehension can mean understanding the order in which events occurred. It can mean literal understanding of what you read or making an inference or a guess about what will happen next or what a character might be thinking based on the information you have read.

> There is more to reading comprehension than just knowing the meaning of each word.

Sometimes having difficulty in one of these areas can affect all three. For example, if you are having trouble sounding out words, that is going to cause you to read at a slower pace. When you are busy concentrating on each word, you may not be thinking about the entire sentence or paragraph. That can make it tough to remember what you just read, or to put it together as a whole. This affects your reading comprehension.

HOW DO KIDS DESCRIBE THEIR READING DIFFICULTIES?

Anna is a 15-year-old student at a public school who describes herself as having mild dyslexia. She and her mom talked about her reading difficulties with us.

How old were you when you realized that you were having trouble with reading? How did you feel about it?

Anna: "Honestly, I didn't realize I was having trouble when I was younger. I thought I was at the same level as the other kids. I noticed late first grade, or early second grade, when I started getting taken out of class. It wasn't until they started pulling me out of class that I realized I was having trouble. Also, when I was very young I wrote backward, from right to left. I can still do that when I want to, and I can read it just fine. In fact, if you take out all the spaces and punctuation in something, I can still read it. That's something a lot of people with dyslexia can do. I have mild dyslexia."

So you probably like texting, right?

Anna: "Yes, because nobody can tell if I spell something wrong."

What makes reading hard for you?

Anna: "My comprehension is very good and always has been. Right now, I have one of the highest reading levels in my class. I just can't read aloud well, and I'm not very good at spelling. I can tell you what the word means if I look at it, but if you take the card away and then ask me what the word is, I can't spell it. My handwriting is also really bad. I write really big, like a fifth grader."

Anna's Mom: "Anna has no phonemic awareness. She knows a word, and can tell you what a word means, but when she reads it or says it aloud, it doesn't come out the same. I'll tell her no, that's wrong, take another look. Then she'll look at it again, and take some more time, and she can get it. She needs longer to process what she's reading, and she works really hard at it."

Other students with reading difficulties who were surveyed online also described what made reading hard:

> **Keith, age 15**: "Lots of things make it hard to read, like having to keep my place and decoding words."
> **Renee, age 15**: "Not being able to understand the context of the story."
> **Adam, age 12**: "Words that I don't know very well and haven't been introduced to yet."
> **Elliot, age 10**: "I find it a little hard, especially long words and big paragraphs."

DO READING DIFFICULTIES EVER GO AWAY?

What makes reading hard for you?

Reading disabilities are a lifelong condition, but that doesn't mean that you'll never be able to learn to read. As you learned in the earlier definition, dyslexia is neurological in origin, which means that it has to do with the way your brain

"Lots of things make it hard to read, like having to keep my place and decoding words."—Keith, age 15

works. Studies have shown that people with dyslexia use their brains differently when reading than people who don't have this disorder. As a matter of fact, several brain studies using functional magnetic resonance imaging (functional MRI, for short) have been conducted on people with and without dyslexia. A functional MRI shows a picture of your brain, with different areas highlighted as they are working. In 2007, in an article entitled, "Dyslexia Begins When the Wires Don't Meet," Mark Roth of the *Pittsburgh Post-Gazette* reported about three such studies that were conducted at Carnegie Mellon University, Georgetown University, and Yale University. (You can see the story at http://www.post-gazette.com/pg/pp/07042/760823.htm.)

What these functional MRIs proved was that people with dyslexia used their brains differently while they were reading than those without dyslexia. There are at least three areas of the brain involved in reading. The Broca's area, named for the scientist who discovered it, is the part of the brain located near the left temple that is responsible for language and speech. Two other areas of the brain that are activated while reading are closer to the back of the brain. Typical readers heavily use a part of their brain involved in phonological awareness, or decoding the sounds of written language, located just above the left ear. Those with dyslexia in the study were less efficient in using these areas of the brain when reading.

The *Pittsburgh Post-Gazette* also reported that as readers become more skilled, additional areas in their brain become active when reading, especially an area in the back of the brain, just next to where visual processing takes place, that contains the memories of whole words. Typical readers are able to use the parts of their brain that process the visual features of numbers and letters like lines and shapes and then connect them to form words and meaning. For those with dyslexia, these connections aren't working as quickly or easily. This doesn't mean that people with dyslexia or reading difficulties aren't smart. In fact, they are often very creative and full of great ideas! You may be surprised to learn that many famous celebrities have dyslexia or other reading difficulties.

So can reading difficulties go away? There are strategies to work around these brain differences and to engage other areas to compensate. Although reading may be something that you will always need to work at, over time you can learn to read accurately and begin to move from learning to read, to reading to learn. You will find out about some of these strategies in Chapter 5. This is why it is so important for teachers to use an approach that works with the way that their students' brains are processing information.

> **People with dyslexia are still smart, creative, and full of good ideas!**

HOW MANY PEOPLE HAVE READING DIFFICULTIES?

The short answer is, a lot! According to the International Dyslexia Association (2008), as many as 15%–20% of the population as a whole has at least some symptoms of dyslexia, which means some difficulty reading, even if it's not enough to have received special education services in school. According to research released in 1994 by the National Institutes of Health (Bright Solutions for Dyslexia, 1998), dyslexia affects at least one out of five children in the United States and is the most common and prevalent of all learning disabilities. (See http://www.dys-add.com/nowknow.html#NIHResults for more information.) Among students who are receiving special education services, the vast majority are identified as having difficulty learning to read. According to the 2002 President's Commission on Excellence in Special Education, that number is two out of every five students. No matter how you look at it, this is not your problem to deal with alone. It affects a significant number of people and is even thought to run in families.

> Dyslexia affects at least 1 out of 5 children in the U.S. and is the most common and prevalent of all learning disabilities. In fact, among kids who receive special education services in school, 2 in 5 have difficulty learning to read.

ARE THERE ANY FAMOUS PEOPLE WHO HAVE DYSLEXIA OR OTHER READING DIFFICULTIES?

If you have difficulty reading, you are in good company. There are plenty of celebrities, artists, scientists, and other famous people who have dyslexia or other reading difficulties. Some of the world's most famous inventors are thought to have been dyslexic, including Leonardo da Vinci, Alexander Graham Bell, and Thomas Edison. Many business leaders have also been identified as having dyslexia, including Henry Ford, Ted Turner, and Charles Schwab. Artists such as Pablo Picasso, Auguste Rodin, and Andy Warhol, musicians including Cher and John Lennon, and filmmakers like Walt Disney all are identified as having had dyslexia or reading-related challenges. And speaking of Walt Disney, you probably didn't realize that two key members of the cast of the Disney movie *Pirates of the Caribbean* are dyslexic—both Orlando Bloom and Keira Knightley. Even some of today's biggest stars, including Tom Cruise, Will Smith, and Usher, have spoken publicly about their dyslexia. Having difficulty with reading didn't prevent any of these people from going on to lead wildly successful lives. It won't stop you, either!

WHAT CAN I DO ABOUT MY DYSLEXIA OR READING DIFFICULTY?

There is plenty that you can do to take control of your reading difficulties. That's what this book is all about! Remember that you are not alone; millions of people have the same difficulty with reading that you do. Don't be embarrassed to ask for help or to use strategies that your friends or classmates might not be using. You are about to learn in the next chapter that it doesn't matter how you get there, only that you learn to read in a way that works for you.

Picture This:
What Is a Reading Disability?

TYPE OF READING DIFFICULTIES

Decoding	Difficulty understanding how sounds relate to the written word and what groups of letters make up which sounds. Also called phonological awareness.
Fluency	Difficulty reading accurately and at an appropriate rate with correct intonation.
Comprehension	Difficulty understanding what you have just read. Comprehension can be literal (the facts) or inferential (making judgments and predictions).

Two out of give children in the U.S. who are receiving special education services have difficulty learning to read.

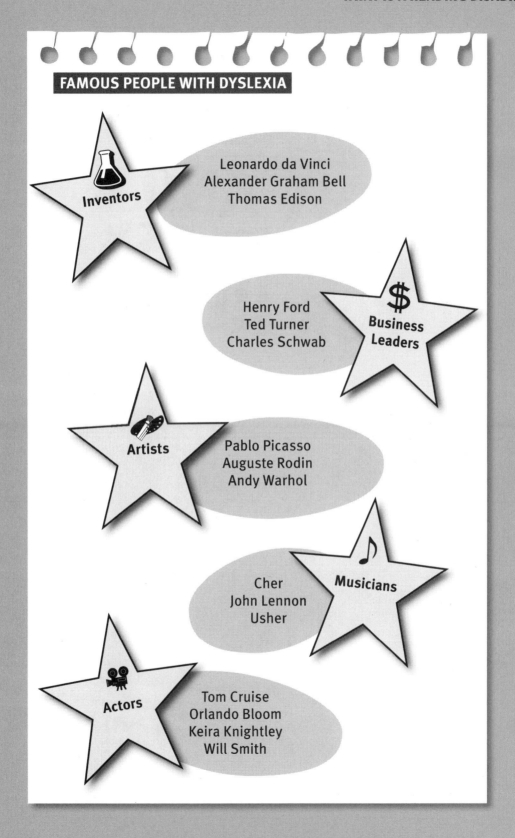

FAMOUS PEOPLE WITH DYSLEXIA

Inventors
Leonardo da Vinci
Alexander Graham Bell
Thomas Edison

Business Leaders
Henry Ford
Ted Turner
Charles Schwab

Artists
Pablo Picasso
Auguste Rodin
Andy Warhol

Musicians
Cher
John Lennon
Usher

Actors
Tom Cruise
Orlando Bloom
Keira Knightley
Will Smith

CHAPTER 3

WHY AND HOW TO ASK FOR HELP

n Chapters 1 and 2, you discovered what it really means to read and what kinds of things might make reading hard for you. The next few chapters will focus on reading strategies, which are like tips and tricks you can use to help make reading easier and more fun. Before you begin, it is important to understand why you need to be able to read fluently and accurately, and that it's okay to need help.

KYLE'S STORY

Kyle is 10 years old. He struggles with reading and has a lot of difficulty with sight words, especially when he doesn't have a lot of time. Kyle didn't really think being able to read quickly was important, until one morning when it snowed outside. As his mother was making breakfast, Kyle looked at the television. Words were quickly scrolling across the bottom of the screen . . . school closings! Kyle tried to figure out if he was going to be able to stay home. The words kept scrolling, and he saw "Mo" at the beginning of one, and a capital "C" right after it. It must be Montgomery County, his school district!

"Mom," Kyle called excitedly, "there's no school today! It's a snow day!" Kyle's mother walked over to the television. "Where does it say that?" she asked. Kyle pointed as "Mo" rolled by once more. His mother shook her head and said, "No, Kyle, that's Morgan County, West Virginia. They must have gotten a lot more snow than us, and they're closed today. Your school is open." Kyle felt terrible. For the first time, he began to wonder if reading could be important for more than just schoolwork.

WHY IS READING IMPORTANT?

Reading is important, and not just for school. It is the key to unlocking the world around you. Reading tells you what's going on and why, how to do things, where to find things, and much more.

When asked, "Why do you think reading is important?" students with reading difficulties had a lot to say.

> **Renee, age 15**: "Without reading you wouldn't be able to get a job or succeed in school or college. Everything involves reading so it automatically makes it important."
>
> **Adam, age 12**: "In life you will have to read books and signs and tests, like your driving test. You will have to read signs like road signs. And you need to study without your parents helping you."
>
> **Robert, age 12**: "I think reading is important to add on to your vocabulary."
>
> **Chris, age 15**: "So people can record things and pass information down through history without things getting mixed up."

On the other hand, not all of the students felt the same way.

Why do you think reading is important?

"In life you will have to read books and signs and tests, like your driving test. You will have to read signs like road signs. And you need to study without your parents helping you."—Adam, age 12

> **Elliot, age 10**: "I don't think reading is important."

Even though you probably know deep down inside that reading is important for many reasons, it might be so frustrating for you that you feel just like Elliot. You may not enjoy reading right now. That's okay. The truth is, as you practice and become more skilled, reading will become easier. When something becomes easier, it becomes more fun to do. That may be the time when you decide to pick up a book and read just for pleasure. In the meantime, it's important to let those around you help you out. Rather than focusing on what everyone else is doing, take pride in the progress that you are making.

Remember when you learned how to ride a bicycle? What happened when your parents took off your training wheels? Were you able to ride like a pro right away? Of course not! It was hard at first. Maybe there were even a few times that you felt like giving up. Then, with practice and hard work, one day it all came together. First your parents held on while you started to ride. Finally you got up on that bike, took off all by yourself, and didn't fall. Faster and faster you rode, and you realized that you could do this. Believe it or not, learning to read is a lot like that.

SELF-ADVOCACY AND SUPPORT IN THE CLASSROOM

In an online survey of students in grades 5–12, students who found reading difficult were asked whether they felt comfortable asking for help. Most said that they were "somewhat comfortable" asking for help, although when asked how often they asked for help from an adult when they didn't understand what they were reading, most answered "sometimes" or "never." Only one student answered "always."

Asking for and accepting help and making those around you aware of your needs so that they can support you is called self-advocacy. It's nothing to be embarrassed about. Being able to explain your needs is a useful skill and one that you will use all the time as an adult. Did you know that as a student with a disability that impacts your education (or makes it so that you are unable to do some of the things your classmates can do in

self-advocacy: asking for and accepting help and making those around you aware of your needs so that they can support you. It's nothing to be embarrassed about.

the same way that they do it), you may be entitled by law to certain rights? Students with disabilities who need special education and related services are guaranteed the right to a free and appropriate public education (also known as FAPE) under the Individuals with Disabilities Education Improvement Act (IDEA) of 2004. This includes specialized instruction, such as in reading or writing, and/or modifications to the learning program to meet your needs. Students with disabilities also have the right to accommodations in the educational program so that they are not unfairly discriminated against because of their disability under Section 504 of the Rehabilitation Act of 1973.

> **Students with disabilities may have the right to accommodations in the classroom.**

What are classroom accommodations? Accommodations are changes to the way your teacher presents information or to the way you are required to complete assignments or take tests, all based on your needs. For instance, you may be allowed to listen to books on tape or use a computer program such as Kurzweil 3000 to assist with your reading comprehension. (You will learn more about these in Chapter 6, when we discuss technology to help with reading difficulties.)

If you need accommodations or specialized instruction to help you make progress with reading, then chances are you have a 504 Plan or an

> **accommodations:** changes to the way your teacher presents information or to the way you are required to complete assignments or take tests, all based on your needs

Individualized Education Program (IEP). If you're not sure, you can ask your parents. A 504 Plan will spell out the classroom accommodations that you are entitled to in order to allow you equal access to classroom instruction despite the impact of a disability. You shouldn't be embarrassed or ashamed about needing accommodations. A student who needs accommodations is no different from a student who needs glasses to see the board. Someone who has trouble seeing the board wouldn't be expected to sit way in the back of the room, or try to see clearly without glasses. It is a way to level the playing field or make things fair for everyone.

An IEP goes a little further than a 504 Plan. Along with listing the accommodations or modifications that you might need, an IEP sets annual goals for progress in your areas of need. Public schools are responsible for designing instruction to help you meet these yearly goals. Private schools are a whole different story and may or may not be covered under these laws depending on whether they receive public funding. However, there are also private schools that specialize in teaching students with reading challenges.

If you are receiving special education services at your school, you are not alone. The Learning Disabilities Association of America reported in an Action Alert in April 2011 that there are nearly 7 million children with disabilities who receive special education services under IDEA. Of these, the 2002 President's Commission on Excellence in Special Education estimates that 40% are receiving special education services to help them read. Can you do the math? About 2.8 million students share your difficulties, and those are only the ones who have been identified and qualify for services. Perhaps millions more have reading difficulties that get in their way, but haven't been officially diagnosed.

MORE FROM ANNA

Remember Anna and her mom from the last chapter? Anna is 15 years old and describes herself as mildly dyslexic. When asked how she felt about asking for help, Anna described it this way:

I'm paranoid about asking for help. I hate doing it. I have a lot of pride, and I don't like being "that kid" who needs help. I was sick of having devices shoved in my face. I wouldn't use an Alpha Smart or spell checkers. I felt like it was cheating. Also, some kids teased me about needing help. One of my good friends stuck up for me, and made them stop.

Anna eventually began to accept help, although mostly in ways that didn't set her apart from other students.

I want to be an actress when I grow up, and I am completely determined to be able to read well. My parents always used to read aloud to me, and I loved that. In third grade, I had a great reading teacher, and I really loved independent reading. I also didn't mind using a scribe, someone who would write down what I told her to. Eventually I learned to type, and that has really helped with my writing.

I also had a tutor who helped a lot with spelling and helped me edit my words for essays. I practiced reading in front of her. She had an endless exercise book, which I dreaded. We also worked with flash-cards. I liked the tutor, and I didn't mind working with her because it was outside of school.

Now I love to read. Reading is an escape from daily life. Reading helped me survive middle school! If I could tell students who are struggling with reading why they should keep at it, I'd tell them to read *The Book of a Thousand Days* by Shannon Hale if they were a girl, or *Holes* by Louis Sachar if they were a boy. I'd say, "See what you you'd be missing if you didn't read?!" *The Book of a Thousand Days* is sophisticated, but not hard. *Holes* teaches you to keep going. These books are gateways. Kids should know about the magnificent worlds that books can bring you to.

HOW TO ASK FOR HELP

As Anna pointed out, asking for help can be hard. You don't want to feel like you are being singled out or look bad in front of your friends or classmates. Here are some ideas about how to ask for help without calling attention to yourself:

➤ Start with your parents. Ask for their help with reading, writing, or homework, and see if they can talk to your teacher to get strategies, which are like tips and tricks you can try at home.

➤ Talk to your teacher before or after school or during lunch. Find some private time when nobody else is around to talk to your teacher about what you find difficult. Ask if he or she has any ideas that might help.

➤ Come up with a signal for your teacher. If you are too embarrassed to raise your hand or ask questions during class, see if you can come up with a special signal just between the two of you to let your teacher know that you need some help.

➤ Participate in homework club, if your school offers it. Some schools have special afterschool sessions for homework or tutoring. These can be very helpful!

Remember, it's not how you get there that matters. It's that in the end, you will be able to read accurately and effectively in your own way and in your own time.

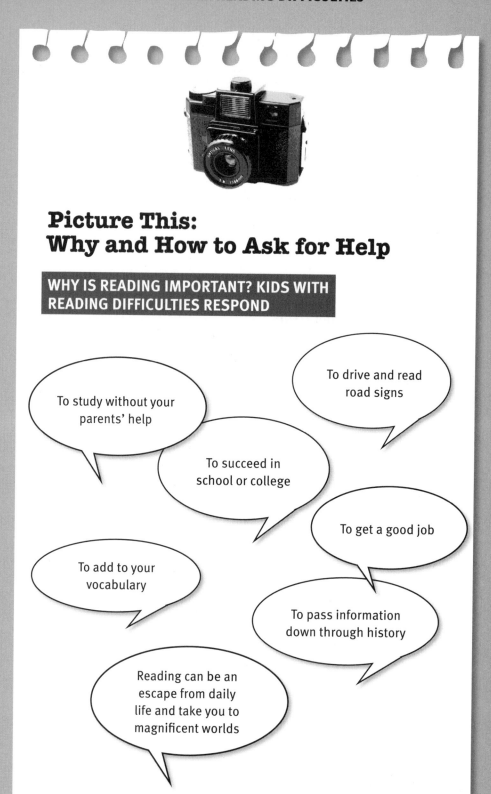

Picture This: Why and How to Ask for Help

WHY IS READING IMPORTANT? KIDS WITH READING DIFFICULTIES RESPOND

To study without your parents' help

To drive and read road signs

To succeed in school or college

To get a good job

To add to your vocabulary

To pass information down through history

Reading can be an escape from daily life and take you to magnificent worlds

HOW CAN I ASK FOR HELP WITH READING?

✔ Talk to my parents

✔ Talk to my teachers during private time, like lunch or before or after school

✔ Come up with a special signal between my teacher and myself that means I need help

✔ Participate in an afterschool homework club

EXAMPLES OF HOW YOUR SCHOOL CAN HELP YOU THROUGH AN IEP OR 504 PLAN

Accommodations	➤ Large print
	➤ A reader
	➤ Books on tape
	➤ Screen reader (such as Kurzweil)
	➤ Notes, outlines, and instructions
	➤ Use of a scribe (someone writing down what you say)
	➤ Use of a word processor
	➤ Speech-to-text software programs
	➤ Respond directly in the test booklet
	➤ Use of a calculator
	➤ Use of a spell checking device
	➤ Use of graphic organizers
	➤ Extended time for tasks and assessments
	➤ Multiple or frequent breaks
	➤ Reduce distractions
Modifications	➤ Reduce written workload
	➤ Provide you with alternative ways to demonstrate mastery
	➤ Reduce the number of problems on a test or quiz
Supplemental Aids and Services	➤ Break long-term assignments down into smaller, more manageable pieces with interim due dates
	➤ Preferential seating
	➤ Use of a pencil grip
	➤ Checking your agenda book daily
	➤ Use of a carrel for independent work
	➤ Use of a specific reading program

CHAPTER 4
HOW I LEARN

E verybody learns differently, and that's okay. It's what makes us special. Think about how boring life would be if we all learned in the same way. Learning styles are just the different ways we learn. They also relate to the different types of intelligences that you will learn more about in this chapter.

Learning styles make us unique.

WHAT ARE THE FOUR LEARNING STYLES?

There are four styles of learning. Can you identify which style describes the way you learn?

➤ *Visual Learners*: Visual learners learn through seeing information. They have an easier time learning when information is presented in pictures, diagrams, or charts. Outline format is exceptionally effective. Students who are visual learners can look at text and form pictures of it in their head, which leads to making the text more concrete. Challenges for the visual learner include having difficulty with oral directions, especially if they require multiple steps. They may also have difficulty when there is outside noise or background music while trying to learn.

➤ *Auditory Learners*: Auditory learners learn best when able to hear, speak, discuss, and think about things out loud. They usually remember information when it has been explained to them orally, like during a lecture. Auditory learners have strong language skills. They can carry on interesting conversations and get their ideas out easily for others to understand. Auditory learners usually have musical talents and have an easier time learning a foreign language. Challenges for auditory learners include when they are expected to comprehend text while reading silently or follow directions that are only in writing.

➤ *Kinesthetic Learners*: Kinesthetic learners learn best by movement. They use their bodies to learn. For example, if a kinesthetic learner is learning short vowels, he might make his mouth in the shape of the letter O while saying the sound. Many kinesthetic learners end up becoming athletes or musicians. There are many challenges if you are a kinesthetic learner. It can be difficult to sit still during a lecture, which makes it hard for you to pay attention to what you are hearing. It also can be a challenge for kinesthetic learners to listen to others or to do independent work in a school setting. Unless you are moving, you will get bored very easily, which will interfere with your learning.

➤ *Tactile Learners*: Tactile learners have the most fun. They learn through hand-on approaches, like touching or experimenting with objects. Sculpting clay into letters to learn their shapes and sounds is an example of tactile learning. It is almost always paired with kinesthetic learning, as tactile learning requires movement. Students who need hands-on learning are usually the fidgeters in the group. They learn better while playing with an object in order to increase their attention.

> **The four types of learning styles are: visual, auditory, kinesthetic, and tactile. Which one are you?**

WHAT IS METACOGNITION, AND WHY IS IT IMPORTANT?

Identifying your learning style is essential. Here is a word that you should learn inside and out. It is probably one of the most important words that you need to know if you have reading difficulties. *Metacognition* refers to the mental processes we use to monitor and regulate our own learning (Flavell, 1976). *Megacognition is the process of thinking about thinking.* An easy definition comes from Merriam-Webster's Dictionary and defines metacognition as an "awareness of one's own learning or thinking process." It is digging deep inside yourself and learning/knowing how you learn best. It is figuring out what type of learner you are and how to apply those skills to your everyday life. For example, if you know that you are a visual learner and you have to study for a social studies test, you would not to ask somebody to record the textbook for you. You know to ask for outlines of the text or to create flashcards for new vocabulary words that you need to know for the test. That is having metacognitive skills.

Understanding your learning profile can also mean recognizing what can make things difficult and when

metacognition: a fancy term for learning about how your learn

you need strategies for help. These three students were able to clearly identify what aspects of reading gave them the most trouble:

Ellen, age 16: "Keeping the words in mind and understanding it."

Shelby, age 14: "Getting into the book makes reading hard for me. This is partly because of my impatient side, and that I would much rather read books that start off exciting, but life isn't always perfect like that."

What aspects of reading give you the most trouble?

"Getting into the book makes reading hard for me. This is partly because of my impatient side, and that I would much rather read books that start off exciting, but life isn't always perfect like that."—Shelby, age 14

Alan, age 17: "It's hard for me because of my trouble with reading comprehension. The books and texts use words that are hard to sound out because they are so descriptive and seem long."

So what does that mean for you? It means that there are different learning strategies for different learners. This chapter will give you the best strategies for learning based on your learning style.

STRATEGIES FOR VISUAL LEARNERS

➤ Ask for directions in writing, especially if they require more than one step.

➤ Ask for an outline of the material being covered during a lecture.

➤ Create flashcards to learn new concepts or vocabulary words.

➤ Ask for a demonstration or illustration of a new concept or skill.

➤ Read new information to yourself before reading it as a class.

➤ Take notes, then go back to edit your notes to filter out the important information. Putting your notes into outline form is especially helpful.

➤ Use graphic organizers.

➤ Ask the teacher to give you additional time to think before answering an oral question. This allows you time to process the information, translate it into picture form, and then get it out orally.

➤ Study in a quiet environment.

➤ Highlight or underline important information in a text.

➤ Doodle. Some parents or teachers may think that doodling may be a distraction, but it can actually help you pay more attention to what you are learning.

If they don't believe you, have them read this chapter on learning styles. It can't hurt!

➤ Draw pictures that represent concepts or vocabulary words.

➤ As you read, make pictures in your head.

STRATEGIES FOR AUDITORY LEARNERS

➤ Use books on tape or eBooks that "talk" to you. Many of them allow you to slow down or speed up the rate of reading. This also makes rereading a lot easier.

➤ Ask to be read to. Being read to is fun at any age.

➤ When you are presented with a worksheet, read it aloud or make sure you listen to the teacher if she is reading it to the class.

➤ Playing background music is effective for auditory learners.

➤ Making up mnemonic devices, such as ROYGBIV (roy-gee-biv) for remembering the colors of the rainbow, is effective. For those who do not remember, it is red, orange, yellow, green, blue, indigo, and violet.

➤ Study aloud with a classmate. Quiz each other.

➤ Form a study group.

➤ Create a song based on information you need to learn.

➤ Use technology. There are many text-to-speech software programs, such as Kurzweil 3000, that allow you to scan in any printed material, then read it back to you.

STRATEGIES FOR KINESTHETIC LEARNERS

➤ Move around while you are studying. It is okay not to sit in the same place for extended periods of time.

You can bounce a ball or read your notes aloud while walking around the room.

➤ Take frequent breaks while studying. Get some exercise or eat a snack.

➤ Reread the text as many times as you can, as your attention span is probably too short to learn large pieces of information in short periods of time. This is called "chunking."

➤ Ask for extended time to take tests. See if you can take tests over multiple days.

➤ Doodle (see the strategies for visual learners).

➤ Highlight or underline text while reading.

➤ Act out new concepts, or make up a dance in order to remember them. For example, if learning how to add double-digit numbers, make up a dance that represents each step.

STRATEGIES FOR TACTILE LEARNERS

➤ Write or draw new concepts or vocabulary words.

➤ Using manipulatives such as Base-10 blocks or math cubes to improve your learning.

➤ Used lined paper with a raised mid-line so you can feel when you are going out of the lines.

➤ See if there are hands-on ways to learn new concepts such as getting sandpaper and cutting out letters. Use your finger to touch each letter while saying its sound.

➤ Get different-colored pencils and make "rainbow words." Take one color and write a word that you need to learn. Then trace over the word using a different color, until you create the rainbow effect.

➤ Spread shaving cream on a table. Use your finger to draw letters into the shaving cream while saying the letter's sound. This is also a great way to learn new spelling words or learn to divide words into syllables.

➤ Take breaks while studying.

➤ Make a model of a new concept if possible.

➤ Paint a picture of the concept you're studying.

WHAT ARE MULTIPLE INTELLIGENCES?

Howard Gardner is a developmental psychologist who is best known for his theory of multiple intelligences. He has come up with nine different types of intelligences, which should be a relief to those with reading difficulties because it lets you know what other strengths you have and how to use those strengths to help you learn more effectively. Remember metacognition?

> **There are many different forms of intelligences, not just ones surrounding reading.**

When you are reading about the different types of intelligences, think about how they are connected to the four different learning styles. Think about which one you fit in. Then you could match the learning strategies not only to your learning style, but to your intelligence type. The different multiple intelligences are (Gardner, 2000):

➤ *Visual/Spatial Intelligence*: You tend to think in pictures and need to create mental images. You can easily use maps, charts, and pictures to help learn. You have many talents such as doing puzzles, painting, and having a good sense of direction. Many people with visual/spatial intelligences become artists, architects, and mechanics.

➤ *Verbal/Linguistic Intelligence*: You have super auditory skills and excellent speaking skills. You think in words instead of pictures. Your skills include story telling, explaining, remembering information, teaching, and understanding the meanings of words.

Those who have verbal/linguistic intelligence go on to become attorneys, teachers, or journalists.

➤ *Logical/Mathematical Intelligence*: You have the ability to use reason, logic, and numbers. You ask a lot of questions and like to do experiments. Your skills include figuring out relationships, doing experiments, doing difficult mathematical calculations, and understanding geometry. Scientists, engineers, computer programmers, and accountants are all jobs of those with this intelligence.

➤ *Bodily/Kinesthetic Intelligence*: You have the physical coordination to control your body movements and handle objects with skill. You express yourself through movement and have good hand-eye coordination. You are able to remember and process information through movement. Careers that use this intelligence include sports, teaching, and acting.

➤ *Musical/Rhythmic Intelligence*: You have the ability to produce and appreciate music. You think in sounds, rhythms, and patterns. You may become a musician, singer, or composer.

➤ *Interpersonal Intelligence*: You have the ability to relate to and understand others. You can see things from other people's point of view. You can understand other people's mood and have the ability to understand both verbal and nonverbal cues. This is exceptionally important in a subject like social studies. You may become a politician or go into business.

➤ *Intrapersonal Intelligence*: You have the ability to self-reflect and recognize your own strengths and weaknesses. You can analyze yourself. A career that involves philosophy could be a possibility.

➤ *Naturalistic Intelligence*: You have the ability to relate to your own natural surroundings and tend to be a nurturer. Two career choices that would work with this type of intelligence would be farming or gardening.

➤ *Existential Intelligence*: You like and enjoy thinking and are very curious about life, death, and everything in between. A career in philosophy may be up your alley.

Let's look at the connection between learning style and multiple intelligences. Let's say your intelligence is in the visual/spatial area. Are you going to learn best by having someone read to you? No. You need to create pictures and mental images to retain information. You would use the strategies of the visual learner. What if you are logical/mathematical? You ask a lot of questions and like to do experiments. You could be either a tactile learner or an auditory learner. Use those strategies to help you learn.

WHAT IS EXECUTIVE DYSFUNCTION, AND HOW DOES IT AFFECT LEARNING?

The term "executive dysfunction" has become very popular in the last decade. Joyce Cooper-Kahn and Laurie Deitzel (2008), authors of *Late, Lost, and Unprepared*, define executive dysfunction as "a set of processes that all have to do with managing oneself and one's resources in order to achieve a goal. It is an umbrella term for the neurologically-based skills involving mental control and self-regulation" (p. 10). What does that mean? It means that those with executive dysfunction generally have difficulty with impulse control, cognitive flexibility, initiation, working memory, planning and organizing, and self-monitoring. Difficulty in any of these areas can affect your ability to begin a task or to stick with it. Here are more details about these areas:

➤ *Impulse Control*: This is your ability to think before you do something. In reading, poor impulse control would affect your ability to maintain focus on the word or sentence you are reading instead of moving on to the next page without really understanding what you just read. Impulse control would also make you guess more quickly at a word without spending time sounding it out and making sure it makes sense in the given context.

➤ *Cognitive Flexibility*: This means how you adapt to new situations and how you handle frustration. This would affect your reading if you found a text too challenging and would affect how you would react to the text. Would you give up or move forward? You would need to change your mind and make mid-course corrections while reading.

➤ *Initiation*: This means your ability to start a task such as homework or projects. For those with dyslexia or other reading difficulties, this is exceptionally difficult. Why would you want to begin a task that you feel is exceptionally hard? But think positive. You can do it!

> **People with executive dysfunction generally have difficulty with impulse control, planning, and organizing, and self-monitoring.**

➤ *Working Memory*: This is your ability to temporarily retain information in your mind at the same time that you manipulate the information in order to use it for a related task. In reading, poor working memory could affect how you learn the alphabet, reading comprehension, solving multistep math word problems, and completing long-term projects. You may have difficulty taking notes or following multistep directions.

➤ *Planning and Organizing*: This refers to your ability to complete long-term projects, budget your study time at home, or turn in your homework. You may end up spending too much effort on one assignment and not enough time on another. In reading, you will see someone who has difficulty with planning and organizing struggle with studying from a text and taking tests.

➤ *Self-Monitoring*: Self-monitoring is the ability to look at what you have just done and reflect on it. For example, you may gloss over a word too quickly and not see that the word you read does not make sense in the text. When you self-monitor, you stop, ask yourself if that word makes sense in what you are reading, then go back to correct that word. You also ask yourself questions while you are reading to make sure you understand the text.

Understanding whether or not you are affected by executive dysfunction is also an important step in understanding how you learn and what kinds of

planning and organizing: the ability to complete long-term projects, budget your study time at home, or turn in your homework

strategies will work best for you. If you know that you have difficulty planning or beginning an assignment or sticking with it once you've begun, then you can plan for that by using the strategies above. Are you a kinesthetic learner? Take frequent movement breaks, and then get back to work! Are you a visual learner? Start organizing your thoughts with a diagram or graphic organizer, and see if that helps to get the ideas flowing. Are you an auditory learner? Tape record your ideas and then play them back to help you do your assignment. Are you a tactile learner? Make use of manipulatives, or things you can touch, as inspiration or reminders to work through projects. Starting to get the idea?

The next two chapters will introduce you to even more reading strategies, as well as assistive technology to help in all of these areas. You are beginning to learn how to take control of your reading and studying challenges!

Picture This!

THE FOUR TYPES OF LEARNERS

Type of Learner	Characteristics
Visual	➤ learn by seeing information in pictures, charts, diagrams, or outlines ➤ can look at text and form pictures of it in their heads ➤ have difficulty with oral directions
Auditory	➤ learn best when able to hear, speak, discuss, and think out loud ➤ usually remember lectures or oral presentations ➤ have strong language and conversation skills
Kinesthetic	➤ learn best by movement ➤ use their bodies to learn ➤ have difficulty sitting still
Tactile	➤ learn through hands-on approaches, like touching or experiments ➤ can increase their attention by holding an object in their hands ➤ often fidget and have trouble paying attention to lectures

STUDY TIPS FOR DIFFERENT LEARNERS

Are you a visual learner? Try this:

➤ make flashcards

➤ use an outline

➤ take notes

➤ highlight important information

➤ draw pictures to represent ideas

Are you an auditory learner? Try this:

➤ use audiobooks

➤ play background music

➤ make up mnemonics

➤ study aloud with a friend

➤ write a song

Are you a kinesthetic learner? Try this:

➤ move around when learning

➤ take lots of breaks

➤ exercise or get a snack

➤ doodle

➤ act out new concepts

Are you a tactile learner? Try this:

➤ use manipulatives (like cubes)

➤ use lined paper with raised lines

➤ trace letters and words with your fingers

➤ use different-colored pencils to mark important ideas

➤ make a model

CHAPTER 5
READING STRATEGIES

As we learned in previous chapters, reading is a very complex system with many steps and parts. Between phonics, syllables, words, fluency, vocabulary, and comprehension, it is a lot to process. Only 80% of our English language follows phonics rules, which means the other 20% have to be memorized.

> **Only 80% of our English language follows phonics rules. The other 20% has to be memorized.**

Some students do not like to ask for help, while others seek out assistance from adults.

Maggie, age 10: "I don't like asking my teacher to help me read the words. I'm afraid she will think I am stupid."

Sam, age 13: "Sometimes I ask my parents to help me with a word, especially if it is in a textbook that I have to read."

Hannah, age 11: "I always ask a teacher to help me sound out a word if I have tried everything else and still don't get it."

Do you ask for help with reading?

"I always ask a teacher to help me sound out a word if I have tried everything else and still don't get it."—Hannah, age 11

Asking for help is a way to begin, but there are also different strategies that students can use independently to help decode words. In a survey of students in grades 5–12, the four most popular strategies they used to help with decoding were:

➤ asking yourself if what you read makes sense in the context of the text,
➤ using context clues,
➤ sounding out the word, and
➤ using illustrations.

> It is *always* okay to ask for help from a parent, teacher, or friend.

LIST OF COMMON STRATEGIES TO HELP WITH DECODING

Here are many other helpful strategies that you can practice in order to help decode words. Try some out and see which ones work best for you!

1. Sound out the word. Use what you know about the six types of syllables and the syllabication rules to help you decode the word.

2. Ask yourself if what you are reading makes sense in the context of the text. It is very common to guess at a word that you don't know based on the first letter or group of letters that you see. Ask yourself, "Does that word make sense?" If you are reading a book about baseball, you will probably come across the word "bat." If you say "bab" instead, ask yourself if that makes sense. Then go back to the word and try a different strategy to sound out the word.

3. Use illustrations if they are available to help you read unknown words or before guessing at a word.

4. Use context clues. Skip the unknown word and go back to it after reading some more of the text.

5. Make sure you know where you are in the text. It is sometimes hard to move from line to line without getting lost. You can use your finger to track the words you are reading or use a highlighting strip, which shows you what you are reading in a different color.

Figure 1 lists the percentage of students who use those strategies to help them decode while reading independently.

There are 44 phonemes (sounds) used to form syllables and words (18 vowels and 26 consonant sounds). Do you know how many words we can make with these phonemes?

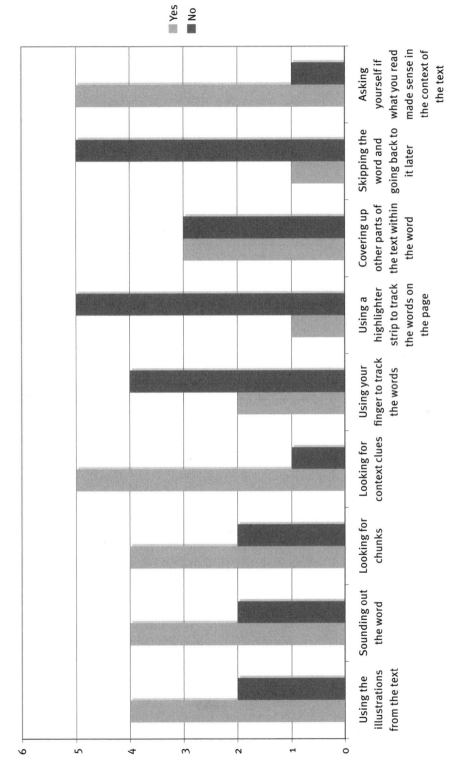

Figure 1. Strategies used by students to help with decoding.

There are way too many to list! A person with a reading disability has trouble connecting a sound to its printed letter, so learning all of the phonemes is the first step. Whoa . . . you don't have to learn all 44 at one time. Let's take it step by step! Many reading programs include the order of phonemes you should learn and the order you should learn them in. It is difficult to give you an order in which to learn your letters and their sounds, as different programs use different orders.

BREAKING DOWN WORDS INTO SYLLABLES

In Chapter 1, we discussed the six different types of syllables. Remember, a syllable is a word or part of a word that has a vowel you can hear. The numbers of vowels you can hear equal the number of syllables in that word.

1. Closed syllables such as in "bat," "cup," and "lip."
2. Open syllables such as in "hi" and "we."
3. Vowel-consonant-e syllables (the magic-e rule) such as in "cake" and "bite."
4. Vowel team syllables are when two vowels next to each other make a new sound such as in "moat," "bleat," and "paint."
5. Consonant-le syllables such as in "able."
6. R-controlled syllables such as in "for," "car," and "sir."

HOW DO I KNOW WHAT TYPES OF SYLLABLES ARE IN THE WORD?

Step 1: Mark the vowels with the letter *v* under each one, using a red pen.

Step 2: Using a different color pen, mark the consonants with the letter *c* under each one.

Step 3: Connect the vowels. Use your red pen to draw loops connecting each of the vowels.

Step 4: Locate the consonant patterns (CVC, VCe, etc.).

HOW WE DIVIDE WORDS INTO SYLLABLES

A syllable is a word or a part of a word with one vowel sound. We use closed, open, r-controlled, diphthong, VCe, and C-le syllables to build all words in our language. Recognizing the syllable types will help you sound out and spell unfamiliar words.

> A syllable is a word or a part of a word with one vowel sound.

Great news! There are just five combinations of vowels and consonant combinations. We learn these rules to make reading easier, so we can break down an unknown word into smaller pieces that we do know. Here is the list you have been waiting for. The V stands for vowel and the C stands for consonant.

➤ VCCV: Divide between the two middle consonants: ban|dit, sup|per. In the word *bandit*, we divided between the *n* and the *d*. The *a* has to sound short because it is "closed in" by the consonant *n*. In the second syllable, the vowel *i* must also be short because it is closed in by the *t*. So after you divide the word, you then have to determine the type of syllable it is. How about the word *invade*? Simple. You would divide the word between the *n* and *v*. The *i* would sound short because it is "closed in" by the *n* and the *a* in the second syllable would sound long because it is a VCe syllable.

☛ Usually divide before a single middle consonant (VCV) such as o|pen and i|tem.

☛ Divide the word before the consonant that falls before the Cle syllable. For example, take the word *able*. Using this rule, you would divide the word between the *a* and *b*. The *a* will sound long because it does not have a consonant to its right to "close it in" and the second syllable will be the Cle syllable.

➤ VV: If there are two vowels together that don't represent a long vowel sound or a diphthong, divide the syllables between the vowels such as in "li|on" and "qui|et."

➤ VCCCV: This usually means that there is a consonant blend in the word. The first thing you should do is circle the blend, then divide the syllable between the blend and the remaining consonant such as in the words "hun|dred" or "sim|ply."

➤ VCCCCV: The four consonants in the middle can either be two separate blends or digraphs or one triple blend of consonants as in the word "hatchling."

LET'S NOT FORGET ABOUT COMPREHENSION

Some decoding strategies, such as using illustrations, are also great comprehension strategies. Comprehension is something many kids with learning difficulties struggle with. Although these students also struggle with comprehension, see if you can spot some potential strategies to be used in their thoughts about understanding what they read:

Michael, age 9: "When I read by myself, I sometimes skip over sentences that I think are too hard for me. Then I don't know what the story is about."

Megan, age 14: "Most of the books I have to read for school don't have pictures so I have to read the same page over and over sometimes before I get what I'm reading."

Simon, age 12: "I don't understand most things I read unless someone reads them to me."

The students above listed three great strategies to help with their comprehension. First, you can skip over things you don't understand, as Michael does, but you should be going back and re-reading them or asking for help with the items you skipped. Second, you could do like Megan does and re-read a piece of text more than once (especially if it doesn't have pictures you can rely on). Finally, like Simon, you can ask someone else to read a section of text you're struggling with to you.

As we read in the previous chapters, there are two types of comprehension, literal (right-there questions) and inferential (why questions.) Here is where it gets a little complicated. You may understand more of a text when it is read to you than when you read it independently. Does that mean you have weak comprehension skills? No. It just means you need to understand how you learn best. There are three types of ways to comprehend text:

➤ listening comprehension, or being read to;
➤ silent comprehension, or when you read to yourself; and
➤ oral comprehension, or when you read aloud.

> **Comprehension refers to how well you understand what you read.**

HOW CAN I IMPROVE MY COMPREHENSION SKILLS?

➤ Increase your vocabulary. From computer programs to good old reliable flashcards, improving your vocabulary will improve your comprehension.
➤ Increase your reading fluency. As your decoding becomes stronger, so will your comprehension.
➤ Use illustrations from the text. If you look at the illustrations both before and during reading, it will make understanding the text easier. This goes along with taking a "picture walk," or looking at the illustrations first, before you start your reading.
➤ Reread, reread, reread! This can't be stressed enough. Many students with dyslexia or other reading difficulties spend so much time decoding that their

comprehension suffers. There is nothing wrong with rereading a passage several times in order to get the meaning. Faster is not always better.

➤ Let somebody read the text to you, get an audio book and follow along in your text, or try an eBook reader.

➤ Stop and ask yourself questions while reading.

➤ Take notes. It is a great strategy to take notes while reading. From using a graphic organizer to help you remember the main idea, characters, and setting, to writing down the important facts from each chapter, taking notes will improve your comprehension.

WHAT ARE SIGHT WORDS?

A sight word is any word that is known by a reader automatically. The reader should not spend more than 3 seconds identifying the word before being be able to move on to the next word. There are many different sight word lists, such as the Dolch Sight Word List and the Fry Instant Word List. There are some upsides to learning sight words. For example, the Dolch list contains 220 words, with 150 of them following traditional phonics rules, so you can initially learn them by sounding them out. By reading those words over and over again, they will become automatic and be part of your sight word vocabulary. Another positive about learning sight words is that they are the most frequently found words in children's books, which means you will see them again and again. That is exceptionally helpful to visual learners.

In Chapter 4 we discussed different learning styles. Knowing your style of learning is important, because that can help you choose a

sight word: any word that is known by a reader automatically

strategy that works for you. Below are lists of strategies to learn sight words based on your learning style.

STRATEGIES FOR LEARNING SIGHT WORDS FOR VISUAL LEARNERS

As a visual learner, there are many strategies you can use to learn sight words, including:

➤ Make flashcards and have someone drill you frequently. Keep a chart of your progress.

➤ Create a shape around each sight word. For example, the word "the" would look like: the

➤ Make two sets of flashcards with the same words on both sets. You can play many games with these cards:

☞ Go Fish: Deal five cards to each player and put the rest face down in the middle. The first person asks the other if he or she has a certain word. If that person does, the card is given to the first player. If that person does not have that card, the first person has to pick a card from the middle pile. The player with the most sets wins.

☞ Memory: Lay the cards face down and choose two. Read both words. If they match, you win the set. If not, turn the cards over and it is the next person's turn. The player with the most sets wins.

➤ Play sight word BINGO: Choose 24 sight words, some you know and some you do not, and put each word on an index card. Then make a blank 5 x 5 grid and randomly place 24 sight words in the spaces, leaving the center as the free space. Make several BINGO sheets, using the same words but in different locations. Put the cards face down. One person picks the word and reads it aloud. If you have that word, cross it off or use a coin to cover it. You can play until you get five in a row or choose to fill up the whole sheet.

➤ Create a word search puzzle on the computer.

➤ Choose 10 words that you are learning. Write each word on an index card and place a piece of magnetic tape on the back of each card. Tie a string to a rope and place a paper clip on the end of the string. Go "fishing" for words. When you get one, read it aloud and keep the card. You can play this by yourself or with others.

➤ Highlight a given sight word in a children's magazine. Say it while you are highlighting.

STRATEGIES FOR LEARNING SIGHT WORDS FOR AUDITORY LEARNERS

Strategies for learning sight words include connecting the printed word to your speaking vocabulary. Some activities to reinforce this strategy include:

➤ Listen to a book on tape and point to each word as it is spoken.

➤ Have an adult give you a sight word such as "the." Search through some books or magazines and identify the word while speaking it at the same time.

➤ Have an adult show you a flashcard of a sight word and have that person say the word. Now you put the word into your own sentence. When you get to the sight word in your sentence, point to the flashcard.

➤ Create a song that includes the sight words you are working on. You can either make up your own tune or use an old familiar tune such as "The Wheels on the Bus."

➤ Say the word aloud, and then say each letter of the word, then the word again. You can use different voices for the letters that you frequently get wrong.

STRATEGIES FOR LEARNING SIGHT WORDS FOR KINESTHETIC LEARNERS

This learning style is a fun one to have when learning sight words.

➤ Act out the sight word and have someone guess the word you are acting out.

➤ Make a hopscotch board and put a different sight word in each box. Say each word as you step on it.

➤ Make a set of sight word flashcards.

➤ Have someone show and say the word to you while you jump rope or hula-hoop.

➤ Put the words down on a Twister™ mat and read each one when you land on that color.

➤ Put the flashcards in two piles across the room from each other. Time yourself to see how fast you can run from one pile to the other, reading each word when you get to that pile.

➤ Write the words on golf balls. Putt the balls into a cup while saying the words.

➤ Write the words on balloons and throw several up in the air. As each one comes down, say that word.

➤ Fidget while studying. You might think you're supposed to sit still while studying, but not if you're a kinesthetic learner! You may actually remember better if you fidget. For example, play with some Silly Putty or keep a small smooth rock in your pocket.

STRATEGIES FOR LEARNING SIGHT WORDS FOR A TACTILE LEARNER

Here are strategies to help you with your sight words by using your learning style to your advantage.

➤ Use clay to form each letter that makes up the word you are working on.

➤ In pencil, write the word you want to learn or have someone write it for you on an index card. Trace over the letters in glue and then put sand on top. Remove the excess sand by shaking off the card, and let it dry. You will have your very own set of tactile word cards.

➤ While reading, follow along with your finger.

➤ Walk around the room while studying flashcards.

➤ Fidget while studying. For example, play with some Silly Putty or keep a small smooth rock in your pocket.

➤ Rewrite the sight words over and over

➤ Put shaving cream on a table and use your finger to write the word in the shaving cream. Whipped cream is also fun!

READING PROGRAMS

There are many different reading programs that address reading issues. For example, if you have a difficult time with decoding, there are special programs out there to help you with that specific problem. There are also programs to help you with your vocabulary, comprehension, and fluency. If you feel that you are having a difficult time learning how to read with the program you are currently using, let your teacher, tutor, or parent know so they can help figure out other options. There could be another reading program that will work better for you.

Picture This

COMPREHENSION STRATEGIES

We polled the kids we interviewed for this book to see what types of comprehension strategies they used to help them read.

**Have you ever used any of the following strategies
to help you understand what you are reading?**

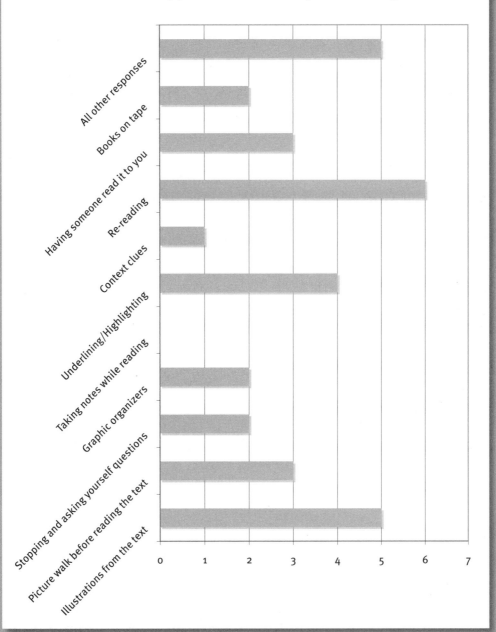

CHAPTER 6

TECHNOLOGY FOR READING AND WRITING

Having a reading disability isn't fun. It certainly is not something you would want if you were given the choice, but it is important to remember that you have a huge advantage in this day and age, compared to just a generation ago. The advantage you have today is the explosion of technology, both hardware and software, that is available to help you. Imagine a world without word processing, spell checker, the Internet, or eBook readers. How much more would you be struggling? Just a few years ago, there wasn't even an iPad. Can you imagine where technology will take us in the next few years?

MAKE SURE THE TECHNOLOGY MATCHES YOUR STYLE

Of course, just because a technology exists doesn't mean it's the right one for you. When we talked with Joan Green, author of the 2011 book *The Ultimate Guide to Assistive Technology in Special Education: Resources for Education, Intervention, and Rehabilitation*, she noted, "The world of technology has become much more affordable: Many cutting edge resources can greatly enhance the quality of life of students who have reading and writing challenges. The key is to figure out which technology is the best match for the needs of each individual."

Before running out to buy the latest gadget or program, you really need to stop and consider whether it suits your personal needs and preferences. Take eBook readers, for example. They can seem like a great solution for certain reading difficulties. Some eBook readers include integrated dictionaries, text highlighting features, and the ability to customize your reading by choosing font sizes and styles or even margin spacing. Others offer text-to-speech features, or the ability to convert books into audio files, which can be very helpful for struggling readers. In its "2010 Kids and

Family Reading Report," the Harrison Group and Scholastic (the company that publishes the Harry Potter series) reported that of the 2,000 kids surveyed between the ages of 9 and 17, 33% agreed with the statement "I'd read more books for fun if I had greater access to eBooks that I could read on an electronic device" (p. 16).

Although there's no denying their usefulness, not everyone is comfortable with eBook readers. Remember our friend Anna, who is 15 years old and has mild dyslexia? Anna has an eBook reader, but she found that it wasn't the best fit for her.

> I have a Kindle and will sometimes use that, but I really don't like it. I like the sense of accomplishment that I get when I finish a big book. When I read on a Kindle, I can't tell where I am in the book. I like books on tape, because I can do other things while I'm listening and it helps me remember.

Anna realized that listening to a book and being able to do other things while she was listening were the best strategies for her learning style. Just as we learned in the last chapter about how reading strategies work best when they match your learning style, the same is true with technology.

It is also important to choose technology that you are comfortable using. Renee, also 15 years old, was embarrassed by using certain types of devices in the classroom, especially those that were meant for younger children. Others were just as helpful and didn't set her apart as much.

> I didn't really like using a device with a headset, because it was embarrassing. I don't like listening to books on CDs at all. Other than that my Franklin spell checker helped me a lot during school to look up words for definitions. If it's a book for school I will read a summary online first. That way if I read the

words wrong I won't get too far off. Plus I will already know the main story and only read for the details.

Fortunately, there are so many different technological devices and programs available that you are sure to find one that is the perfect fit.

Choose technology that you are comfortable using. For example, Renee, age 15, said, "I didn't really like using a device with a headset, because it was embarrassing." Her spell checker, however, was a tool she was comfortable using at school.

TECHNOLOGY FOR READING (DECODING)

Although there are some high-end programs available to help with reading, sometimes simple technology works well, too.

➤ *Audiobooks* are a great way to help build reading skills. Try listening to the book as you're reading along. A great source for audio books is Learning Ally, formerly known as Recording for the Blind and Dyslexic. Membership is free for qualified families and allows access to literally thousands of recorded books. You can find these at http://www.learningally.org.

➤ *eBook readers*, mentioned above, can highlight text and change fonts and margins, and some even have text-to-speech capability. There are literally dozens to choose from, so be sure to search the web and compare and contrast features to meet your needs. Think about whether you prefer e-ink or LCD; grayscale or color; WiFi connectivity; screen size; and availability of titles. Some of the more popular devices include:

☞ *Amazon Kindle*: http://www.amazon.com
☞ *Barnes and Noble Nook*: http://www.barnesandnoble.com
☞ *Sony eReader*: http://ebookstore.sony.com/reader

➤ The *iPad* has made a big splash when it comes to revolutionizing assistive technology and making it inexpensive and accessible. There are thousands of apps that are useful for those with reading difficulties, and more are being created every day. Many are free or just a few dollars to download. Some examples included below cover phonics and text-to-speech apps or those that read books aloud on your iPad. Be sure to browse http://www.apple.com/education/apps to find many more:

> There are thousands of iPad apps to address difficulties with reading and writing, with more being created every day.

- ☞ *abc PocketPhonics by Apps in My Pocket*: http://www.appsinmypocket.com
- ☞ *FirstWords: Deluxe by Learning Touch*: http://itunes.apple.com/us/app/firstwords-deluxe/id337462979?mt=8
- ☞ *SuperWhy! by PBS Kids*: http://itunes.apple.com/us/app/super-why!/id357422351?mt=8
- ☞ *Speak it! Text to Speech by Future Apps Inc.*: http://itunes.apple.com/us/app/speak-it!-text-to-speech/id308629295?mt=8
- ☞ *vBookz Free Audiobooks by Mindex International Ltd*: http://itunes.apple.com/us/app/vbookz-free-audiobooks/id366703930?mt=8

SOFTWARE THAT WORKS ON YOUR COMPUTER

➤ *Kurzweil 3000* is a well-known software program for those who need help reading and writing. Your school may even have it available for you to use. You can download text in digital format or scan it into the program, which will read it aloud, adjusting the rate to your comfort level, highlight words or sentences as you go along in various colors, take notes, and even develop a study guide. You can find it at http://www.kurzweiledu.com.

➤ *Simon S.I.O.* is a program offered by the Don Johnston Company that has individualized phonics instruction for beginning readers, as well as activities for spelling and fluency. Simon S.I.O. can be purchased from http://www.donjohnston.com.

➤ *WordMaker* is another program that provides systemic phonics instruction to build spelling and decoding skills. It can be purchased from the same company as Simon S.I.O. at http://www.donjohnston.com.

➤ *Reader Rabbit* is a software program that has long been a favorite of many families. The company offers software featuring learning games for various grade levels, up to grade 9, and two phonics-based products for beginning readers:

  ☞ Reader Rabbit Learn to Read With Phonics for kindergartners

  ☞ Reader Rabbit I Can Read With Phonics for first and second graders

The Reader Rabbit software programs can be purchased from http://www.reader-rabbit.com.

➤ *Headsprout* offers online programs and products to teach early reading and comprehension for grades K–5. Check out its programs at http://www.headsprout.com.

> If you're feeling overwhelmed by all of the information on technology tools, flip to the Resources section at the back of this book. It has a simplified list of each of the technology tools we talk about in this chapter.

TECHNOLOGY FOR
READING COMPREHENSION

Many of the devices and programs listed in the previous pages to help with reading skills can also help with reading comprehension. Strategies such as isolating small areas as you read, having the text read aloud to you, or electronically highlighting and being able to link to word pronunciations and definitions are also useful to help understand what you are reading.

In addition, there are a number of online sites, software programs, and iPad apps that can help develop reading comprehension skills. Here is just a small sample of what's available:

➤ *Readability* is a web and mobile app that works in a browser to isolate words and simplify the way you view text. It can also sync with the Kindle. You can find it at http://www.readability.com.

➤ *Simple English Wikipedia* uses fewer words and easier grammar than the regular English Wikipedia. This can help struggling readers understand difficult topics. Go to http://simple.wikipedia.org to view this site.

➤ *Into the Book* is a free online site that teaches essential strategies for reading comprehension, including visualizing, summarizing, synthesizing, making connections, using prior knowledge, inferring, evaluating, and questioning. You can access this site at http://reading.ecb.org.

➤ *Mr. Nussbaum* is a popular Internet site created by a teacher. It is filled with learning strategies and practice exercises for all subjects. By clicking on the Language Arts icon, you can access printable reading comprehension passages for grades 3 and up. Find this site online at http://www.mrnussbaum.com.

➤ iPad apps are also available to help with reading comprehension.

☛ For younger students, *Question Builder by Mobile Education Tools* is designed to teach kids how to answer abstract questions and create responses based on inferences with why, what, where, how, and random question formats. For more information on this app, visit http://mobile-educationstore.com/ipad-apps or look on the iTunes app store.

☛ For the older student, *Shakespeare in Bits by Mindconnex Learning Ltd.* offers animated editions of selected Shakespeare titles, and larger speeches are broken up so that the highlighted area corresponds to the animation. For more information on this app, visit http://www.shakespeareinbits.com/sibsite or look on the iTunes app store.

TECHNOLOGY FOR WRITING

In the next chapter, you will learn about the relationship between reading and writing. If reading is challenging for you, it follows that writing can also be a difficult task. There are two areas where technology can help. Technology can help with the physical act of writing, if you find writing with a pencil and paper difficult or tiring. Technology can also help with the organizational part of writing, or getting your thoughts down on paper in a way that will make sense to your audience. Let's explore the benefits of computers and word processors first.

COMPUTERS, WORD PROCESSORS, AND OTHER DEVICES

Technology with built-in word processing program features can be extremely valuable. These features allow you the freedom of making mistakes while writing and the knowledge that you can edit later, which can help with the flow of writing and assist in written output. Your stress level will decrease when you take grammar and other common writing errors out of the picture. This is a safety net. If you are thinking of purchasing a computer for this reason, make sure you look at all of the options, including a laptop.

The better you are at keyboarding, the more useful computers will be. If you are not a very good typist, there are a number of programs that can help you develop this skill. Some of the popular keyboarding/typing programs include:

➤ *Type to Learn*: http://www.sunburst.com
➤ *Dance Mat Typing*: http://www.bbc.co.uk/schools/typing
➤ *Typing Adventure*: http://www.typingadventure.com
➤ *GS Typing Tutor*: http://www.typingstar.com

If a computer or word processor is not available, other options exist. A separate spell checker device is less expensive and more portable. It can sit on your desk at school and fit in your backpack to take home. Some students who have a computer at home use the spell checker device at school. Some examples of these devices include:

➤ *Children's Speller and Dictionary*: http://www.franklin.com
➤ *Webster's Spelling Corrector Plus*: http://www.franklin.com

Other devices, like the NEO or DANA, have the benefits of a word processing program but are less expensive and more portable. They are compatible with many Palm OS education applications as well. They can be set up to store each subject area in a separate location. All of the information that you input can be downloaded to a computer. These devices only let you see a limited number of lines at a time, which could be a downside when writing.

The iPad can be an option for portable word processing as well, although some may find the touch screen keyboard more difficult to use than a traditional keyboard. If that's the case, then a Bluetooth keyboard case may help. This type of iPad case includes a touch keyboard that works wirelessly with your device. Some examples include:

➤ *RightShift Bluetooth Keyboard Case*: http://www.solid lineproducts.com/ipad/ipad-keyboard-case-config. html

➤ *Logitech Keyboard Case by Zagg*: http://www.zagg.com/ accessories/logitech-ipad-2-keyboard-case?gclid=CL OYrfvKnasCFQHf4Aodvgryiw

WORD PREDICTION AND MIND-MAPPING TO HELP WITH THE WRITING PROCESS

Writing is complicated. The process can be long because it involves brainstorming, prewriting or drafting, using the draft to produce a cohesive written product, and then editing. Don't you wish there was a magic wand you could wave to instantly take your thoughts and transfer them to a written product? Assistive technology can be your magic wand.

Word processing programs offer a variety of methods to organize your writing. They create outlines, including numerals and bullets, so you can get your thoughts down and then manipulate them as needed. These programs allow you the freedom to cut and paste your sentences or paragraphs if you need to change the order of events, and allow for lots of flexibility. The most popular word processing programs are those designed for Microsoft (Microsoft Word) and for Apple (Pages).

If you have difficulty finding the correct word to use, a word prediction software program is the way to go. This type of program works with word processors and also predicts the word a person wants to enter into the computer. A person types the first letter of a word he is looking for and the program comes up with a list of possible words that begin with that letter. If you know the first few letters of the word you are writing, it can predict more complicated words by using yours as the root. Word prediction software also includes assistance with spelling, grammar, and syntax. Some helpful word prediction programs include:

➤ *Co:Writer 6* word prediction software that works with your word processer and also in conjunction with your e-mail. You can purchase it at http://www.donjohnston.com.

➤ *WordQ* uses word prediction, highlighting, and auditory feedback to assist with the writing process. This software can be found at http://www.goqsoftware.com.

➤ *WriteOnline* is a program that you can upload from a CD or log into from the Internet so that it is available anywhere you need it. It offers word prediction and a wide range of additional features such as word banks, read aloud capability, and graphic organizers. For more information on this program, please visit http://www.cricksoft.com/us/products/tools/writeonline/default.aspx.

Mind-mapping software is an amazing tool to help students organize their thoughts and then have the computer generate a written product based on their ideas. Programs such as these allow students to express themselves, either orally or by typing into the computer. Thoughts from the brainstorming process transfer to an outline format to work from. This feature is included in the WriteOnline program mentioned above. Other great programs that can help organize your ideas into a cohesive written product include:

➤ *Inspiration*, *Kidspiration*, and *InspireData* all create graphic organizers on your computer, and with the click of a mouse transform the graphic organizers into outlines. InspireData is used for science, math and social studies and is a visual way to explore and interpret data. You can find all three of these software programs at http://www.inspiration.com.

➤ *Draft:Builder 6* breaks down the writing process into easy steps: brainstorming, note taking, and writing the first draft. It can be purchased from http://www.donjohnston.com.

TEXT-TO-SPEECH AND SPEECH-TO-TEXT TECHNOLOGY

Just like audiobooks or read-aloud programs (also known as text-to-speech features) can help you understand what is printed on the page, some computer programs can also read your writing back to you so that you can hear your errors. There are also programs and features known as speech-to-text technology that allow you to dictate your ideas and let the computer do the writing. Once your thoughts are in the computer via a word processing program, they can be edited as necessary. The following programs offer text-to-speech and speech-to-text:

➤ *Kurzweil 3000*, a program that was highlighted under the Reading (decoding) section of this chapter, can also read aloud scanned or downloaded text and store voice notes.

text-to-speech features: when a device reads aloud to you

speech-to-text features: when the device writes the words that you say

You can buy this program by visiting http://www.kurzweiledu.com.

➤ *Write:OutLoud 6* is a talking word processor that can be used on both Macs and PCs. It confirms word choices with a talking spell checker, homophone checker, and dictionary. It can be purchased from http://www.donjohnston.com.

➤ *WordQ SpeakQ* is a software bundle that includes the WordQ word prediction software detailed above and adds the SpeakQ speech-to-text program by allowing you to dictate your thoughts or type the words you know how to spell and use the speech-to-text feature for the ones you don't. This combined program can be found at http://www.goqsoftware.com.

➤ *Dragon Naturally Speaking* uses voice recognition to enable you to write documents and e-mails, search the web, and control your PC by speaking. More information on this program can be found at http://www.nuance.com/for-individuals/by-product/dragon-for-pc/index.htm.

➤ *MacSpeech* is a company that offers a variety of speech-to-text and other assistive programs, including Dragon Naturally Speaking, for Mac. You can learn more about this company's products by visiting http://www.macspeech.com.

Picture This!

CHOOSING ASSISTIVE TECHNOLOGY DEVICES

How can you choose from the many assistive technology devices available? Draw a chart like this one to help you decide!

```
                                    ┌─────────────────┐
                                    │ speech-to-text  │
                                    │    programs     │
                                    └─────────────────┘

┌──────────────────┐                ┌─────────────────┐
│ Difficulty getting│               │  mind-mapping   │
│ thoughts on paper │───────────────│    software     │
└──────────────────┘                └─────────────────┘

                                    ┌─────────────────┐
                                    │  tape recorders │
                                    └─────────────────┘
```

With today's assistive technology and software, you have a huge advantage over students who had reading difficulties in the past.

CHAPTER 7
THE CONNECTION BETWEEN READING AND WRITING

This chapter focuses on the difficulty some students may face when asked to write. From handwriting, to spelling, to getting your thoughts on paper, writing can be hard and emotionally draining. Teachers may not be able to read your handwriting, especially when there are letter reversals or when your spelling is poor. It is very common for students with reading difficulties to also have problems with writing.

There are many challenges a student with dyslexia might face regarding writing such as:

➤ planning and organizing thoughts,
➤ handwriting,
➤ spelling,
➤ capitalization and punctuation, and
➤ editing.

PLANNING AND ORGANIZING YOUR THOUGHTS

Sometimes the hardest part about writing is just figuring out what to say.

Amanda, age 12: "My teacher puts a topic on the board and then tells us to write about it. I have no idea where to start but am too embarrassed to raise my hand for help. How do I take a topic and turn it into a paragraph?"

Ethan, age 11: "It is hard to pick an idea and find details that go with your idea."

What's the hardest part of writing for you?

"It is hard to pick an idea and find details that go with your idea."—Ethan, age 11

How many times have you stared at a blank piece of paper, not knowing what to write? This is a common problem for students with dyslexia and/or executive functioning difficulties. For example, your teacher puts up on the board, "Write a paragraph about what you did last summer." This is a common writing prompt given to students in the beginning of the school year. Remember, you have not had any writing practice over the summer, yet you come to school the first day back and are now required to write! That can be very stressful.

Take this scenario: You are given a writing prompt and are allowed to choose any format, such as an essay, play, or song, to answer the prompt. Even though you are allowed to choose the format, it can still be difficult to begin the assignment. Many teachers may think that because you are allowed to choose your product, you will not need any help organizing the information. More often than not, you will still need to organize your thoughts, which is why strategies are needed.

One strategy is to create a graphic organizer, such as a story map, to help organize your thoughts. Use the type of graphic organizer that works for you. You can find some examples of graphic organizers in the Picture This section at the end of this chapter. Another strategy is to use assistive technology. As you discovered in Chapter 6, there are also computer programs that allow you to type in key words and the program puts them into outline or paragraph formats such as Inspiration (http://www.inspiration.com). Inspiration uses both pictures and words to create a web. Icons allow the web to turn into either an outline or essay. Another method would be to go right to the computer to get all of your thoughts out, typing them into a word processing document as they come to you. Then you can cut and paste your ideas into the correct sequence. You have to find out which method works for you. Remember, there is no "one size fits all" format to organize one's thoughts.

The truth is, writing can be made more manageable when broken down into easy-to-understand steps. For example, did you know that there are many types of writing? Writing to inform, to persuade, and for personal experience are the three most common reasons we write. By recognizing the purpose of your writing, you have jumped the first hurdle. One mnemonic device that can be helpful in deciding why you are writing is FAT-P:

> ➤ **F**orm: Are you writing a letter, essay, advertisement, or poem?
> ➤ **A**udience: Who is your audience? If you are writing a letter, who do you expect to be reading it?
> ➤ **T**opic: What is the main idea?
> ➤ **P**urpose: Are you writing to inform, to persuade, or to express personal ideas?

We write to inform, to persuade, and to express personal ideas.

HANDWRITING

Handwriting is an extreme challenge for students with dyslexia. It is not uncommon to get a bad grade on an assignment because the teacher cannot read your handwriting. It is either too large, too small, not spaced properly, or just plain old messy. But that is not how it looks to you. You do your best, but still your handwriting looks like a 5-year old did your work for you.

First of all, you need to explain to your teacher how difficult writing is for you. Sometimes it is so difficult that you can't even read your own writing. You have many letter reversals such as a *b* for a *d* or a *p* for a *q*, but that is okay.

WHAT IS DYSGRAPHIA?

The National Center for Learning Disabilities (2010) defined dysgraphia as "a learning disability that affects writing, which requires a complex set of motor and information

DOES THIS LOOK FAMILIAR?

The mite gold biger

Ones a Pon a time ther was
a gold biger. How had a bonky
naoned Spers he was alwas
mad tell he got his ots. The
gold biger fond no gold
and the Porsan that wonts to
boy the mind is coking to bay.
On top of that he had
no more ots to give to Spers.
So the Bonke was ferces. So
wen he got on the bonke
in the mind and he gave
hima Kike he bango.. him →

in to the Seling of the mind
and up ther vas a Pawnd to
a Bono of gold he was so happy
he mooved SPerd the angre bonke
and gave him a wake
he brok the rake and ther
was more gold then he
has ever sen in his life.
P.s. he is fifte Seven
yers old.

Most teachers will tell you that the first step to writing is planning what you are going to write about, which is true. When you look at this sample, you know that this student knew exactly what she was going to write about. Do you think that was easy? When you look at this sample, you see an amazing storyteller, a creative person, and a person with dyslexia. The author, age 11, did not let that stand in her way of writing this story. You notice that all words are spelled phonetically and that the errors are consistent throughout the sample. The letters are reversed and some letters were omitted. That did not stop this student from getting her fantastic story down on paper. Way to go!

processing skills" (para. 1). It makes it hard for a person to see forms and shapes in letters and to understand the relationship between written letters, spoken words, and sound. What does that mean? It means that dysgraphia makes writing difficult. Common problems for students with dysgraphia include difficulties with:

➤ spelling,
➤ poor handwriting, and
➤ putting your thoughts on paper.

Before your hands touch your pencil or keyboard, there are a couple of items you should definitely have in order to help you plan out your assignment. The first is a rubric or outline of what is expected of you for this writing project. The second is a self-editing checklist to use during the revising stage.

Once you are ready to sit down and write, some strategies that can help you with your handwriting are:

➤ A handwriting method such as Handwriting Without Tears™, which can teach you strategies to make the physical process of writing easier.
➤ Use of a pencil grip.
➤ A copy of the alphabet in front of you to refer to.
➤ Special handwriting paper with a raised mid-line (it looks like regular paper).
➤ Use of graph paper to help line your numbers up correctly for math problems.
➤ Use of assistive technology such as a word processor, spell checker, or even a tape recorder to dictate your responses and transcribe them later.
➤ Determine whether you do better by printing or writing cursive. This will make a huge difference with your legibility.

SPELLING

Because your visual memory is weaker than the memories of those without dyslexia or reading problems, spelling poses an additional problem. It prevents you from being able to remember what words look like, even when you see the same words over and over again. Like with reading, there are words that follow common spelling patterns, such as "i before e except after c," as in the words "friend" or "believe." But, as with most rules, there are always exceptions such as in the words "weird" or "their." Unfortunately, you will have to memorize those words that are exceptions to the rule. Words in which you can hear all of the sounds, the ones you can probably decode, will be the easiest words to spell correctly. However, that may not always be true—you may write, "eny" for "any" or "kat" for "cat."

Morgan, a fifth grader, was required to write a conclusion paragraph. Her writing was limited, as it only contained three brief sentences, while her peers had written six within the same period of time. She looked around and covered her work. Her spelling was poor and her handwriting was difficult to read. For example, Morgan wrote, "i tkld abot" for "I talked about." The word "similarities" took up half the line and was spelled phonetically as "smilartes." Her finished product did not answer the given question.

Does this sound familiar?

There is an ongoing debate on whether or not students with dyslexia should rely on spell checkers to correct their spelling errors. "Spell checkers provide a way to self-monitor typos but only if the user can recognize the correct spelling; spell checkers do not help poor spellers generate correct spellings" (Beringer et al, 2008, p. 13).

CAPITALIZATION AND PUNCTUATION

We all know the rules. You always capitalize the beginning word in a sentence. We always capitalize proper nouns such as names of people, states, and other important words. We know to end a sentence with a period and a question with a question mark. When you are writing, those rules seem to float out the door, leaving you with upper- and lowercase letters mixed together and punctuation marks everywhere they are not supposed to be. This is where the editing process comes in.

EDITING

It is difficult to edit your own work when it looks correct to you. Luckily there are tools out there to help you edit your work. What does it mean to edit? You are looking for errors in your writing. Anything from spelling and grammar, to if what you wrote will make sense to the reader—these are all parts of the editing process. The question is, do you know what to look for? There are several ways to edit your work.

First, there is peer-to-peer editing, where someone reads your work and makes corrections and suggestions. There is also teacher editing, where your teacher takes the primary role in marking corrections. The final way is the use of a self-editing checklist or a rubric. A rubric is a list of expectations the teacher has of your work. It covers the content of what should be in your writing as well as reminds you of other areas such as spelling, grammar, and punctuation. Self-editing checklists are more general. For example, you would use a self-editing checklist more for reminders of capitalization, punctuation, and grammar than for the content of the final product.

One common rubric you will see was developed from the 6+1 Trait® Writing program, published by Education

Northwest. This rubric shows scores from 1 (low) to 5 (high) on the following:

➤ ideas (such as a narrow topic and specific details);

➤ organization (such as a clear beginning, middle, and end that make sense to the reader);

➤ voice (whether the writing is interesting, informative, and engaging to the reader);

➤ word choice (using verbs and nouns correctly and whether the words and phrases work well);

➤ sentence fluency (the way the words and phrases flow throughout the text);

➤ conventions (spelling, grammar, usage, punctuation, and capitalizations); and

➤ presentation (consistent and uniform handwriting, good balance of space and text, pleasing overall appearance).

As you can see, this type of rubric is generic, meaning it can be used to score different types of writing, but is effective when looking at the big picture. Your teachers will likely give you more specific rubrics for the assignments they have created.

rubric: a tool used by teachers to let the students know what is expected from them in an assignment

Another great tool to help with your writing is using a self-editing checklist (see the Picture This section on p. 94 for one you can use). It really just is a visual reminder of all of the grammar, punctuation, and capitalization rules that you may have a hard time remembering. The nice thing about using a self-editing checklist is that you can use the same one across all of your classes and for a variety of writing tasks.

You may feel like writing is laborious and hard to do, but always remember that there are ways you can work around your disability to actually become an accomplished writer. You are very creative, but may have problems with your organization or spelling. That should not prevent you from showing everyone how smart you are.

Picture This!

BEFORE YOU BEGIN WRITING

What is the assignment?

_____

_____

_____

_____

What questions need to be answered?

_____

_____

_____

_____

What is my main idea?

_____

_____

_____

_____

What are the supporting details/evidence that support the main idea?

_____

_____

_____

_____

SELF-EDITING CHECKLIST

I started my sentences with capital letters.	
All of my sentences end with the correct punctuation such as a period or question mark.	
I used quotations if appropriate.	
Proper nouns all begin with capital letters.	
All my sentences have correct noun+verb agreement.	
I do not have any run-on sentences.	
I started my sentences with different words.	
I underlined all words that just didn't look right to me to check the spelling of the words.	
I read my essay out loud and it makes sense to me.	

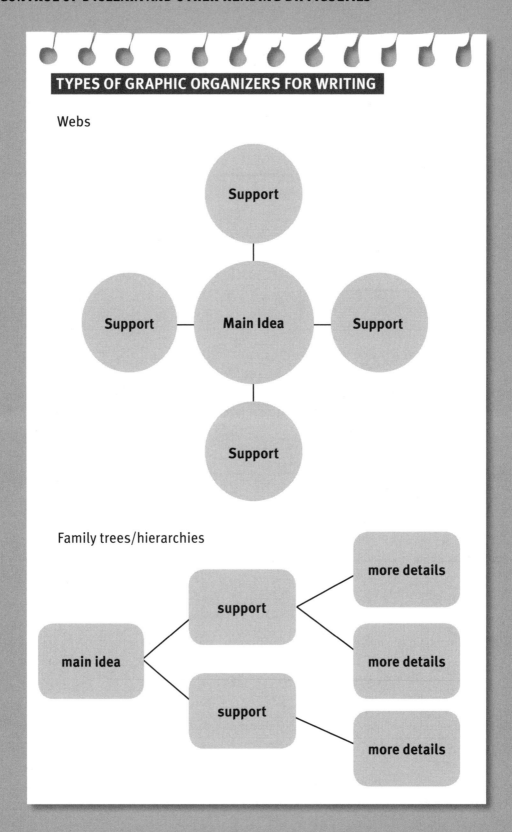

TYPES OF GRAPHIC ORGANIZERS FOR WRITING

Webs

Family trees/hierarchies

Venn diagrams (great for comparing and contrasting things)

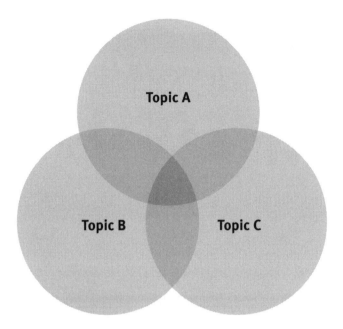

Topic A

Topic B

Topic C

CHAPTER 8
TAKE CONTROL

ow that you've read or listened to the entire book, hopefully you've learned all about:
➤ the steps involved in reading,
➤ what it means to have dyslexia or another reading disability,
➤ how and why to ask for help,
➤ how you learn,
➤ how to match reading strategies with your learning style,
➤ how technology can help with reading and writing, and
➤ how reading and writing are connected.

How are you going to remember all of this information and use it? That's what this chapter is for. Don't worry, there won't be a test. Instead, this chapter is full of questions to remind you of the most important concepts from the book. The questions are arranged by chapter, so if you come across some information that you'd like to review or don't remember reading about, you can turn back to that chapter for more information. Also, if there's something that you've learned and will remember for the future, you can go ahead and check it off the list. It's time to take control of your dyslexia or other reading challenges, and you can do that with information, self-advocacy, and strategies that work together with the way you learn.

CHECKLIST FOR CHAPTER 1: WHAT DOES IT MEAN TO READ?

If you can answer these questions about the reading process, you've learned the basics about what it means to read. If you can't answer a question or don't remember reading about it, don't worry—just turn back to Chapter 1 for more information.

❑   What are the three main purposes of reading?

_____

_____

_____

❑   What are the five essential elements of reading?

_____

_____

_____

_____

_____

❑   What is a genre?

_____

_____

_____

❏ What is your favorite genre? (Trick question! It's not in the chapter, only you have the answer!)

_____

_____

_____

❏ Do you know the six different types of syllables?

_____

_____

_____

_____

_____

_____

❏ What are blends, digraphs, and diphthongs?

_____

_____

_____

❏ What are prefixes, suffixes, and roots?

_____

_____

_____

If you can answer all of the above questions, congratulations! You probably know almost as much as your teacher about what it means to read.

CHECKLIST FOR CHAPTER 2: WHAT IS A READING DISABILITY?

When something gets in the way of one of the steps of reading so that you are unable to learn in the same way that your classmates do, that is called a reading disability. Having a reading disability doesn't mean that you'll never be able to read, and it definitely doesn't mean that you aren't smart. Can you answer these questions about reading disabilities? If not, you can find out more by going back to Chapter 2.

❏ What is dyslexia? You don't need to remember the long, formal definition, but can you remember a few facts about it?

_____

_____

_____

❏ What are the three categories of reading disabilities?

_____

_____

_____

❏ Do reading disabilities ever go away?

_____

_____

_____

❏ How many people have reading disabilities? (You don't need to name an exact number, but do you know whether it is a few or a lot?)

_____

_____

_____

_____

_____

❏ Are there any famous people with dyslexia or other reading difficulties? What are some of their names?

_____

_____

_____

_____

_____

_____

_____

If you can answer these questions, you are on your way to understanding more about yourself.

CHECKLIST FOR CHAPTER 3:
WHY AND HOW TO ASK FOR HELP

Many students are uncomfortable asking for help. They feel like it's embarrassing. The truth is that any new skill takes practice and support. You couldn't ride a bicycle without someone showing you how or without starting off with training wheels. Believe it or not, reading is a lot like that, too. To read more about how other kids with reading disabilities feel about asking for help, turn back to Chapter 3. In the meantime, see if you can answer these questions.

❑ Can you identify two reasons why learning to read is important? (Using your own reasons is fine.)

_____

_____

_____

_____

❑ What is self-advocacy?

_____

_____

_____

_____

_____

❑ What are classroom accommodations, and why might you be entitled to them?

_____

_____

_____

_____

❑ This chapter lists a few different ways to ask someone for help. Can you think of one way to ask for help that would be comfortable for you?

_____

_____

_____

_____

There is no shame in asking for and accepting help when you need it. A student who needs extra support is no different from a student who needs glasses to see the board. Someone who has trouble seeing the board wouldn't be expected to sit way in the back of the room, or try to see clearly without glasses. It is a way to level the playing field, or make things fair for everyone. If you've learned this skill, it will help you throughout your entire life.

CHECKLIST FOR CHAPTER 4: HOW I LEARN

There are many different ways in which people learn. There are also many different types of intelligences. Do you remember what they are? If you don't remember the answers to the questions on this checklist, check out Chapter 4.

❑ What is a visual learner?

_____

_____

_____

❑ What is an auditory learner?

_____

_____

_____

❑ What is a kinesthetic learner?

_____

_____

_____

❑ What is a tactile learner?

_____

_____

_____

❑ Can you name three of the nine different types of intelligences?

_____

_____

_____

❑ Can you figure out what type of learner you are?

_____

_____

_____

❑ What is executive dysfunction, and how might it affect your learning?

_____

_____

_____

❑ Can you name some study strategies that match up with your learning style?

_____

_____

_____

Metacognition is the term for understanding about how you learn, which is what this chapter was all about. Having this self-awareness is very important so that you don't waste your time trying strategies that don't match up with your learning style and therefore won't be effective.

CHECKLIST FOR CHAPTER 5:
READING STRATEGIES

Although asking for help is one very important way to take control of your reading difficulties, there are also a number of strategies that you can try on your own, and they are listed in Chapter 5.

❑ There are four strategies listed in the beginning of this chapter to help with decoding. Have you tried any of them?

_____

_____

_____

_____

❑ Do you know how to break a word down into syllables?

_____

_____

_____

❑ Can you name three strategies to help with reading comprehension? Have you tried them out?

_____

_____

_____

_____

_____

❏ What are sight words?

_____

_____

_____

_____

❏ Did you identify whether you are a visual, auditory, tactile, or kinesthetic learner? Have you checked out the strategies for learning sight words that match your learning style?

_____

_____

_____

_____

_____

These useful tips can make a big difference in helping you learn to independently address your reading challenges. Try them out on your own. You have nothing to lose!

CHECKLIST FOR CHAPTER 6:
TECHNOLOGY FOR READING AND WRITING

Although having a disability is not fun, there are many technological advantages in this day and age that simply didn't exist even a few years ago. Chapter 6 helped to explain the different types of devices and programs available to help with reading and writing challenges at school or at home.

❏ Before considering any technology, have you thought about whether or not it really matches your needs?

_____

_____

_____

❏ Do you know what kinds of features to look for when considering eBook readers?

_____

_____

_____

❏ Are you aware of iPad apps and websites that can help with phonics?

_____

_____

_____

❑ Do you know what kinds of devices and programs can help you with reading comprehension?

_____

_____

_____

❑ Do you use a word processor to write? What about a separate spell checker device?

_____

_____

_____

❑ Are you able to type quickly and accurately?

_____

_____

_____

❑ Do you know what mind-mapping software is?

_____

_____

_____

❑   Do you know the difference between speech-to-text and text-to-speech features?

_____

_____

_____

When used correctly, assistive technology can be just like a magic wand that instantly transforms many of the areas in which you struggle.

CHECKLIST FOR CHAPTER 7:
THE CONNECTION BETWEEN
READING AND WRITING

This chapter focused on the difficulties some students may face when they are asked to write. From handwriting, to spelling, to getting your thoughts on paper, writing can be hard. Are there strategies to help? You bet. If the questions from the checklist aren't ringing a bell, just turn back to Chapter 7.

❑ Do you know why you are writing? FAT-P can help you identify the purpose of your writing. Do you remember what FAT-P stands for?

_____

_____

_____

_____

_____

❑ Besides technology, what kinds of strategies can help with handwriting? For example, have you tried special paper or grips?

_____

_____

_____

_____

_____

❑ What is a self-editing checklist? Can you use the example or develop a rubric that will work for your writing?

_____

_____

_____

_____

_____

When a student has trouble reading or decoding words, he or she often has difficulty encoding or spelling the words, too. Add handwriting difficulties and problems getting your ideas on paper, and the task of writing can seem overwhelming. It doesn't have to be that way. The low-tech strategies in Chapter 7 can provide everyday assistance for this complicated task.

TAKING CONTROL

Change doesn't happen overnight, but by learning and practicing the strategies in this book, you will begin to take control of your reading challenges. Use these checklists whenever you want to remind yourself about all of the different approaches that are available for you to try.

REFERENCES

Beringer, V. W., Nielsen, K. H., Abbott, R. D., Wijsman, E., & Raskind, W. (2008). Writing problems in developmental dyslexia: Under-recognized and under-treated. *Journal of School Psychology, 46,* 1–21.

Bright Solutions for Dyslexia. (1998). *What we now know.* Retrieved from http://www.dys-add.com/nowknow.html#NIHResults

Cooper-Kahn, J., & Dietzel, L. (2008). *Late, lost, and unprepared: A parents' guide to helping children with executive functioning.* Bethesda, MD: Woodbine House.

Flavell, J. H. (1976). Metacognitive aspects of problem solving. In L. B. Resnick (Ed.), *The nature of intelligence* (pp. 231–236). Hillsdale, NJ: Erlbaum.

Fletcher, J., Lyon, G. R., Fuchs, L. S., & Barnes, M. A. (2007). *Learning disabilities: From identification to intervention.* New York, NY: The Guilford Press.

Gardner, H. (2000). *Intelligence reframed: Multiple intelligences for the 21st century.* New York, NY: Basic Books.

Green, J. (2011). *The ultimate guide to assistive technology in special education: Resources for education, intervention, and rehabilitation.* Waco, TX: Prufrock Press.

Harrison Group, & Scholastic. (2010). *2010 kids and family reading report: Turning the page in the digital age.* Retrieved from http://mediaroom.scholastic.com/kfrr

Individuals with Disabilities Education Improvement Act, Pub. Law 108-446 (December 3, 2004).

International Dyslexia Association. (2002). *What is dyslexia?* Retrieved from http://www.interdys.org/FAQWhatIs.htm

International Dyslexia Association. (2008). *Dyslexia basics.* Retrieved from http://www.interdys.org/ewebeditpro5/upload/BasicsFactSheet.pdf

Learning Disabilities Association of America. (2011). *News-in-brief action alert: IDEA survey.*

National Center for Learning Disabilities. (2010). *What is dysgraphia?* Retrieved from http://www.ncld.org/ld-basics/ld-aamp-language/writing/dysgraphia

National Institute of Child Health and Human Development. (2000). *Report of the national reading panel. Teaching children to read: An evidence-based assessment of the scientific research literature on reading and its implications for reading instruction* (NIH Publication No. 00-4769). Washington, DC: Government Printing Office.

President's Commission on Excellence in Special Education. (2002). *A new era: Revitalizing special education for children and their families.* Retrieved from http://www2.ed.gov/inits/commissionsboards/whspecialeducation/reports/index.html

Roth, M. (2007, February 11). Dyslexia begins when the wires don't meet. *Pittsburg Post Gazette.* Retrieved from http://www.post-gazette.com/pg/07042/760823-114.stm

Seipel, S. (2010). *Reading and the brain.* Retrieved from http://www.suite101.com/content/reading-and-the-brain-a303369

Shaywitz, S. (2003). *Overcoming dyslexia: A new and complete science-based program for reading problems at any level.* New York, NY: Vintage Books.

RESOURCES

GENERAL RESOURCES FOR PARENTS AND TEACHERS

Dyslexic Advantage—http://dyslexicadvantage.com
International Dyslexia Association—http://www.interdys.org
Learning Disabilities Association of America—http://www.
   ldanatl.org

Cooper-Kahn, J., & Dietzel, L. (2008). *Late, lost, and unpre-
   pared: A parent's guide to helping children with executive func-
   tioning.* Bethesda, MD: Woodbine House.
Eide, B. L., & Eide, F. F. (2011). *The dyslexic advantage:
   Unlocking the hidden potential of the dyslexic brain.* New
   York, NY: Penguin.

Fletcher, J., Lyon, G. R., Fuchs, L. S., & Barnes, M. A. (2007). *Learning disabilities: From identification to intervention*. New York, NY: Guilford Press.

Green, J. (2011). *The ultimate guide to assistive technology in special education: Resources for education, intervention, and rehabilitation*. Waco, TX: Prufrock Press.

Huston, A. M. (1992). *Understanding dyslexia: A practical approach for parents and teachers*. Lanham, MD: Madison.

Minskoff, E., & Allsopp, D. (2003). *Academic success strategies for adolescents with learning disabilities and ADHD*. Baltimore, MD: Brookes.

Shaywitz, S. (2003). *Overcoming dyslexia: A new and complete science-based program for reading problems at any level*. New York, NY: Vintage.

Tovani, C. (2003). *I read it, but I don't get it: Comprehension strategies for adolescent readers*. Portland, ME: Stenhouse.

West, T. G. (2009). *In the mind's eye: Creative visual thinkers, gifted dyslexics, and the rise of visual technologies* (2nd ed.). Amherst, NY: Prometheus.

Wisniewski, R., Padak, N. D., & Rasinski, T. V. (2011). *Evidence-based instruction in reading: A professional development guide to Response to Intervention*. Boston, MA: Pearson.

ASSISTIVE TECHNOLOGY RESOURCES

AUDIO BOOKS

Learning Ally—http://www.learningally.org

EBOOK READERS

Amazon Kindle—http://www.amazon.com
Barnes and Noble Nook—http://www.barnesandnoble.com
Sony eReader—http://ebookstore.sony.com/reader

IPAD APPS

abc PocketPhonics by Apps in My Pocket—http://www.appsin mypocket.com

FirstWords: Deluxe by Learning Touch—http://itunes.apple. com/us/app/firstwords-deluxe/id337462979?mt=8

Question Builder by Mobile Education Tools—http://mobile-educationstore.com/ipad-apps

Shakespeare in Bits by Mindconnex Learning Ltd.—http://www. shakespeareinbits.com/sibsite

Speak it! Text to Speech by Future Apps Inc.—http://itunes. apple.com/us/app/speak-it!-text-to-speech/id308629 295?mt=8

SuperWhy! by PBS Kids—http://itunes.apple.com/us/app/ super-why!/id357422351?mt=8

vBookz Free Audiobooks by Mindex International Ltd—http:// itunes.apple.com/us/app/vbookz-free-audiobooks/id 366703930?mt=8

COMPUTER SOFTWARE

Co:Writer 6—http://www.donjohnston.com

Draft:Builder 6—http://www.donjohnston.com

Headsprout—http://www.headsprout.com

Inspiration, Kidspiration, InspireData—http://www.inspiration. com

Kurzweil 3000—http://www.kurzweiledu.com

Reader Rabbit—http://www.reader-rabbit.com

Simon S.I.O.—http://www.donjohnston.com

WordMaker—http://www.donjohnston.com

WordQ—http://www.goqsoftware.com

Write Online—http://www.cricksoft.com/us/products/tools/ writeonline/default.aspx

SPEECH-TO-TEXT

Dragon Naturally Speaking—http://www.nuance.com/for-individuals/by-product/dragon-for-pc/index.htm
MacSpeech—http://www.macspeech.com
WordQ+SpeakQ—http://www.goqsoftware.com

TYPING PROGRAMS

Dance Mat Typing—http://www.bbc.co.uk/schools/typing
GS Typing Tutor—http://www.typingstar.com
Typing Adventure—http://www.typingadventure.com
Type to Learn—http://www.sunburst.com

SPELLING DEVICES

Children's Speller and Dictionary—http://www.franklin.com
Webster's Spelling Corrector Plus—http://www.franklin.com

HELPFUL WEBSITES

Into the Book—http://reading.ecb.org
Mr. Nussbaum—http://www.mrnussbaum.com
Simple English Wikipedia—http://simple.wikipedia.org

ABOUT THE AUTHORS

Jennifer Engel Fisher is the Assistant Director of Weinfeld Education Group. She earned her bachelor's degree from the University of Maryland, Baltimore County, and her master's degree in Special Education from Johns Hopkins University. Jennifer taught for 6 years in Howard County, MD, working both as a special education inclusion teacher and self-contained teacher serving a variety of populations including persons with ADHD, learning disabilities, Asperger's syndrome, and students with emotional disabilities.

Jennifer worked for 2 years at a private school in Washington, DC, as a learning specialist consulting with teachers to support students with a wide variety of special needs. She serves as an advocate for students in elementary through high school. One of Jennifer's specialties is organizational coaching for students, especially those with executive functioning difficulties. She also consults with schools, providing them with methods of meeting the needs of their student populations by providing them with training on effective instructional strategies and methodologies.

Jennifer is a contributing author to *School Success for Kids With ADHD*. She is the coauthor of *Take Control of Asperger's Syndrome: The Official Strategy Guide for Teens With Asperger's Syndrome and Nonverbal Learning Disorders*. Both books are with Prufrock Press. Jennifer lives with her husband and two children outside Washington, DC.

Janet Price is the Director of Related Student Services at Weinfeld Education Group, LLC, an educational consulting firm in the Washington, DC, area. She is the parent of two teenagers, one of whom is twice-exceptional—that is, both gifted and learning disabled. Janet holds a bachelor's degree in international affairs from The George Washington University. After a decade of service in the U.S. State Department, Janet found a new use for her skills in diplomacy and negotiation as she began to advocate for services in the public school system for her child's little-understood learning profile. As an educational consultant, Janet now helps other families do the same. She especially enjoys empowering kids and their parents by helping them to understand their learning differences and use their areas of strength to compensate for areas in which they struggle. Janet is the coauthor of the award-winning book *Take Control of Asperger's Syndrome: The Official Strategy Guide for Teens with Asperger's Syndrome and Nonverbal Learning Disorder* (Prufrock Press). Janet lives with her husband, two children, and an overweight Shih Tzu in suburban Maryland.